PICTURES,

PAINTERS,

and YOU

PICTURES,

PAINTERS,

and YOU

BY RAY BETHERS

PITMAN PUBLISHING CORPORATION

NEW YORK · LONDON

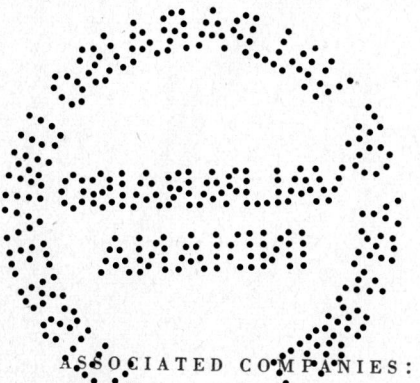

ASSOCIATED COMPANIES: SIR ISAAC PITMAN & SONS, LTD.,

LONDON · MELBOURNE · JOHANNESBURG · GENEVA

SIR ISAAC PITMAN & SONS (CANADA), LTD., TORONTO

PRINTED IN THE UNITED STATES OF AMERICA

Preface

I<small>N THE WRITING OF</small> this book, I owe much to all artists, from prehistoric times to the present day. Of the individuals most responsible for the points of view expressed, my friend Glenn Wessels has perhaps contributed most. Morris Davidson has also been helpful in clarifying certain ideas which follow.

I also wish to thank the Museum of Modern Art, the Metropolitan Museum of Art, the National Gallery of Art, the New York Public Library, the Frick Collection, the Kraushaar, and many other galleries for their cooperation. Also the many private collectors who gave permission to reproduce their paintings. Durand-Ruel have also been most kind in making available their photographic record of Impressionism.

My thanks go to John Rewald, Erle Loran, and Sidney Janis for the use of their motif photographs, and last, but not least, I wish to thank the many artists who have put aside their brushes to describe their own paintings in words.

R<small>AY</small> B<small>ETHERS</small>
New York

CONTENTS

PICTURES,

PAINTERS,

and YOU

"I am here on behalf of my own profession, and I trust it is with no intrusive spirit that I now stand before you; but I am anxious that the world should be inclined to look to painters for information on painting."

John Constable (*1776-1837*)

English landscape painter

Why Should Pictures Need Explaining?

WHAT YOU SEE in any picture always depends on how you look at it, as in the illusion above—while you see a wine glass in one way, you can also see two girls' heads in another. In this case it doesn't much matter which way you look at it, but when you see a work of art, without some compensation, then it's time to do something, to eliminate the "blind spot" that prevents the full enjoyment of *all kinds* of pictures.

There is at present too wide a gap, a lack of understanding between the artist and most people who look at pictures. No one has, so far, satisfactorily explained an artist—how he comes into being; nor has it been explained how an artist will continue to produce creative work in the face of continued lack of support and understanding.

There is no dearth of works of art in the world, but for some reason a great many people deprive themselves of the pleasure of experiencing (that is, appreciating) any work of art. Let us not here become concerned with the appreciation of art as "culture"; what matters more is your own inner satisfaction. Everybody likes pictures up to a certain point, but beyond that point usually comes dislike or disdain, rather than an enjoyed effort to seek and find better understanding. Yet here is the secret—it is in this adventure of seeking and finding that true appreciation lies. And it is not static; it grows with you as you are also growing. As Moholy-Nagy once said, "Art is the senses' grindstone, sharpening the eyes, the mind and the feelings."

So what is it that prevents more people from enjoying pictures as works of art; is it the pictures, the people, or just plain misunderstanding?

I sincerely believe it is the division of pictures, informational or emotional, that is most generally misunderstood. This division is not always clearly marked, for it is sometimes possible to get both information and emotion from the same picture—it is for you to discover what you may *expect* from any picture. But, broadly speaking, informational pictures have long been used to illustrate *other* ideas; things possible to see and to describe in words, pictures as imitations of things. Pictures of this kind are readily understood by everyone; in fact, they are not usually seen as pictures at all but only as substitutes for the objects shown. Informative pictures have a definite factual value, but why exclude the emotional qualities found in other kinds of pictures? To seek information only, in pictures, is much like requiring music to be only the imitation of natural sounds. It is the similarity in the enjoyment of both music and emotional pictures that this book is about—an examination of both kinds of pictures, and of *you*, as you look at pictures.

It is easily possible to have seen pictures all one's life without ever seeing one emotionally, as a work of art. But even so, it is well to remember that all art can never be for all people.

It is the nature of a picture to be experienced as a whole, simultaneously, and not by parts in consecutive time, as are both literature and music. But this book must necessarily be part words, and page must follow page in unfolding the seeing of pictures. For this reason, many single qualities of painting must be considered one at a time (in contrast to painting itself), and one idea must follow another. This limitation makes explanation difficult, for to adequately explain pictures in words several chapters should be read simultaneously, which is of course impossible. As a result, some explanations will seem incomplete until clarified on succeeding pages. Even a second reading of the book might be suggested to overcome the handicap of the consecutive character of words.

As art is a very personal thing, it cannot exist for you at all if not personally experienced, and the greatest satisfaction will be found in making discoveries for yourself. Even in going through this book, you should continually question the ideas presented and weigh them in relation to your own feelings and experience. Some pictures that follow are obviously not works of art, and are purposely included for comparison and study. A few of these are pointed out, but some are not. But I believe that almost any picture has some value, even if only as a stepping stone to the appreciation of more profound works.

No statement on art can be absolute; an artist can always break any rule previously set down. But many principles have appeared again and again, in the painting of all ages, and many of these recurring principles are demonstrated on the pages that follow, where pictures are taken apart, examined and sometimes put together again. At other times, this reassembly of pictures is left to *your* creative imagination, for the enjoyment of art, like everything else, is not gained without some effort on your part. Even your ability to read was not acquired without effort.

Pictures Came before Words

THE CAVE MAN's pictures, after 20,000 years, can still be read by anyone, whatever his language. These pictures of the hunt, bison, mammoths, or reindeer, are remarkably well drawn by any standards. They show great variety in themselves as works of art, and were not pictographs in any sense, to be repeated time after time.

Pictographs developed much later, when pictures became symbols and were arranged in sequence to convey increasingly complicated ideas. Such picture symbols had to be memorized; their meaning as language was entirely dependent on previous mutual agreement and could no longer be universally understood. In addition, the pictograph's message was often far different from what the picture itself might have said.

Pictographs were not only pictures of objects, but often pictures of ideas, words, or parts of words. Each idea, action, or object required its own symbol, and as these grew in number, reading and writing became increasingly more difficult.

Pictures completely disappeared from writing in many languages, supplanted by letters as symbols of only *parts* of words. By this change, the number of symbols was not only greatly reduced, but remained constant. This development simplified writing, if not understanding; for although letters themselves have remained relatively few, the words made from letters have never ceased to multiply.

Cave Painting: Mammoths, Cavern at Font-de-Gaume. *Photograph courtesy of The American Museum of Natural History*

Dakota Indian Pictograph

ABCDEFG
HIJKLMN
OPQRSTU
VWXYZ

What Are Words?

IN OUR everyday use of words, we seldom stop to consider words in themselves, as symbols with no meaning whatsoever. Definitions, as handed down to us, exist only by mutual agreement; "dog" might well have been "cat," had it so happened.

As S. I. Hayakawa * says in his book, *Language in Action,* "No word ever has exactly the same meaning twice. The context—words used in combination—determines the ultimate definition; gesture, facial expression, tone of voice and, in addition, the use of rhyme or rhythm give further variety. It is not only *what* is said, but *how* it is said, that determines final meanings in both words and pictures."

Webster's Dictionary defines the word "cube" as "the regular solid of six equal square sides." This is quoted here in contrast to the twenty-four pictorial "definitions" shown opposite. All are slightly different, but each says "cube" in its own way. It would be virtually impossible to accurately describe these twenty-four cubes in words, words and pictures having so little in common.

Words, as part of a *time* art, line up in a parade, with smaller ideas growing into larger ones on a "string of time." On the other hand, pictures are a *space* art; first impressions are simultaneous, larger areas seen first, with details emerging later.

* *Language in Action,* by S. I. Hayakawa. Harcourt, Brace & Company, New York.

Variation in Word Meanings

Aₛ ᴡᴇ ᴀʟʟ ᴋɴᴏᴡ, many words conjure up mental pictures; but the same word may not produce the same picture for different people. Individual backgrounds, points of view, and all manner of conditions account for these variations.

As an imaginary experiment, suppose we have three people of widely divergent interests: an attractive girl of nineteen, a clown, and a fighter in the heavyweight class. We now ask them, as part of our experiment, to tell us what picture they visualize on hearing the word "ring."

Variation in Picture Meanings

As our same three people now look at this picture of Niagara Falls, the girl's first thought might be "honeymoon" —a natural enough reaction.

The clown is a bit more unpredictable, but he is a showman, after all, so what would be more natural than for him to imagine going over the falls in a barrel—a short cut to fame and fortune before now.

The fighter, resting between bouts, has just begun to read a newspaper with this picture on the front page. But does he look at the picture? Not at all! He turns directly to the sports section, where his real interest lies, and doesn't even see the picture.

Photograph courtesy of Convention and Visitors Bureau, Niagara Falls, N.Y.

Pictures as Information

SOME PICTURES are entirely informational, and like informative writing, are an important part of learning and living. Art is not a "copy of nature," but informative pictures should be copies as far as is possible.

A map, for instance, is a conventionalized picture which stands for a specific geographical territory. If it is not an accurate "copy of nature," then it is of no use whatever. It is also incomplete in itself, as many informational drawings are, until words are used to complete the picture. Its function is to show how to get from here to there, rather than to evoke emotional response.

Another "copy of nature" is found in any pilot book—a drawing of the coastline, for instance. Inaccuracy here may cause a pilot to wreck his ship by relying on inaccurate pictures of unfamiliar surroundings. Botanical and scientific drawings, of all kinds, must also be absolutely accurate, to be of value in their respective fields.

Photography, as a copy of nature, has made its greatest contribution in instantaneously recording events, places, or things. The very knowledge that it *is* a photograph adds authenticity to a picture of this kind. This photograph of a church, for instance, is a substitute for the real church, a fact, which we recognize as being in existence somewhere. But we do not know where, until identifying words complete the picture. And unless this church is known to the observer, or he has some special interest in it, the picture will evoke no feeling but only the fact.

Not all pictures inform; some may offer other things. Music never informs—when someone sings *All God's Chillun Got Shoes,* the "facts" are entirely irrevelant, and are not to be relied upon.

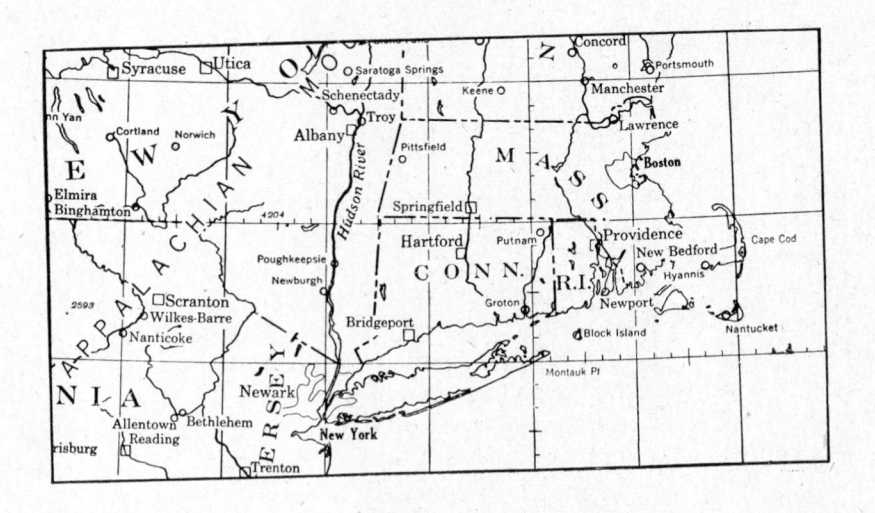

Church in Sonoma, California

How We See

Looking is not always *seeing*, which requires the use of all senses plus past experience. Scanning usually takes the place of seeing with most adults, a casual glance giving just enough information for everyday use.

Sensory impressions are subject to great variation in everyone, with one sense usually dominant. Some people react chiefly to what they hear, and will prefer music to painting, while others will be more responsive to sight, and their preferences will be exactly the reverse. Even where seeing is the stronger sense, hearing, touch and all other senses will be combined in the actual seeing process.

Any picture is always made up of three parts: the artist, the picture, and the observer; all are of equal importance in communication of this kind. The observer will always gain in experience in direct proportion to what he has to give; his capacity to see is almost as important as the artist's ability to paint. To reverse an old saying, "We like what we know"; in other words, we understand what we are looking at.

Seeing can easily be learned, like any other skill. This fact has been demonstrated many times in acquiring knowledge of the relation of mind to sight. Given normal vision, from then on, seeing is primarily a mental process; the eyes act only as lenses for the transmission of light from the world outside.

A wartime example of training in the visual field, from my own experience in Naval Recognition, has a direct relationship to all seeing, in life, pictures or any visual experience. It is outlined here, not as a method, but as a demonstration of learning to see. During World War II, men with all sorts of backgrounds were taught to shoot, and recognition training set out to teach them what, or what not, to shoot at. With little previous experience, these men had to be taught to recognize instantly all types of aircraft, as well as ships, by total form alone; in other words, exactly what these ships and planes looked like.

The original Army system was based on memory; on combinations of wings, engines, fuselage, and tail. But this system was not successful, as words translated into vision were much too complicated to remember.

[14]

The successful Naval Recognition method was developed by Dr. Samuel Renshaw and his associates at Ohio State University, from many previous experiments in optical psychology. Fundamentally, it was based on the theory, "you cannot see what you do not know," and was entirely visual, as opposed to the Army's reliance on remembered words. Recognition had to be instinctive and instantaneous, operating much as a friend is recognized in a crowd. The friend is seen and recognized, without reflection as to how or why. This system forced maximum seeing, during training, by flashing pictures of airplanes on a screen, with successively shorter exposures. The exposure, as identification improved, was shortened to 1/100 of a second, which permitted no time for comparison of one part of the form with another, but forced maximum attention on the form as a whole. With over 100 airplanes to identify, remembered words had already been found inaccurate and cumbersome, as compared to visual memory. Pilots, aircrewmen, gunners, and others were trained in this way and provided with visual memories of countless aircraft and ships that they had never actually seen. It was not uncommon for pilots to name 40 airplanes out of 40, with exposures at 1/100 of a second, from slides selected from over 3,000 different views.

It would be difficult and unnecessary for the individual to follow a system like this, but it does indicate that more intensive seeing can be taught.

To a child, his world is filled with countless *new* things to see, and each one is naturally a new experience. His first view of a tricycle, for instance, with no previous memory of its function, might be only three round forms and some curious angles. Although out of reach, the child will still attempt to reach out and touch it, not yet having learned that depth perception is only part vision, and part memory of having traveled a similar distance before. He then crawls until he can actually touch this new thing; tastes it with his tongue, and bangs it on the floor to see what kind of noise it makes. Then he spins a wheel—a new discovery—and pushes the tricycle along. All these experiences are new and different, and he has discovered them all for himself. It may still be necessary, however, to teach him that a tricycle is made to ride upon. But once he has ridden his tricycle, and learned its name, he will never again see it with the same fresh vision of exploration. From then on, he will see it through use, through its function, rather than in purely visual relationships.

As we all grow up, this fresh viewpoint becomes dulled, and seeing becomes a habit, used for naming things rather than for actually *seeing* them. It remains for artists—who have retained that childlike ability to see things in themselves, and for themselves—to give back to others a fresh viewpoint on things scanned but no longer really seen, of new relationships of form rather than habit relationships of use. Artists do not try to paint what is already seen, but endeavor to point out new ways of seeing.

Seeing has become a habit when the name or use stands for the visual memory of things, or when a specialized interest blinds one to other unseen qualities. To illustrate, suppose our cousin Emma has a new dress, and we prepare to take her picture. We focus carefully on Emma and her new dress, and with the sun behind us, we snap the shutter. But it is only later, when the picture is finished, that we see what hadn't been seen before—the telephone pole which now protrudes from cousin Emma's head. Our specialized interest in Emma and the new dress had prevented our seeing the pole at the time the picture was taken.

On the next few pages, seeing has been theoretically divided into four parts: practical, specialized, reflective, and pure seeing. Not that one kind of seeing is unrelated to another, but this division may help to clarify the way we see. Jan Gordon * and Ralph M. Pearson † have both written on kinds of seeing, and what follows represents, in general, a continuation of their points of view.

Practical Seeing

This is protective, instinctive, the kind of seeing used in quickly stepping aside to avoid being run down by a car. Even lifting one foot after the other in climbing stairs is instinctive, and not usually the result of conscious visual effort and conscious response to a visual stimulus.

Specialized Seeing

Previous interests and training greatly affect this kind of seeing, and can either intensify an image or lessen its visual impression. A bridge of structural steel seen by an engineer, an African chief, and a ballet dancer could hardly appear the same to all three.

How often have we heard the expression, "But it isn't true to nature!" This implies a knowledge of what nature looks like, which, of course, varies with each individual. The bare brown hills of California are considered by some to be very beautiful, but a farmer might prefer green hills—the bare hills, not being productive, would have no beauty for him.

* *Modern French Painters,* by Jan Gordon. John Lane, London, 1923.
† *How to See Modern Pictures,* by Ralph M. Pearson. The Dial Press, 1925.

Reflective Seeing

Things remembered condition this kind of vision. Seeing a picture of a barefoot boy with a fishing pole over his shoulder might start a long chain of reflections, such as "Long ago, when we went fishing with Uncle Ben, who met us at the station and drove us to the farm. He had an old dappled mare with a straw hat, how odd she looked," and so on.

A picture, in reflective seeing, does act as a spur to the imagination, but starts a train of thought that may soon have no relation to the original subject. In other words, a glance has been enough to make us remember other things while we forget the picture completely.

Pure Seeing

This is the field of the artist: to see without relation to use, self, or other nonvisual considerations. This kind of seeing does not refer to "what does it look *like?*" but to "how does it actually look?"

An automobile in *practical* seeing is only a menace to life and limb, to be avoided, and is naturally only partly seen in so doing. In his *specialized* seeing of this same automobile, an ignition expert might immediately look under the hood to investigate his real interest, the ignition system, without ever seeing the car as a whole. *Reflective* seeing could bring memories associated with an earlier car of the same make, memories which replace the thing seen.

But *pure* seeing is an experience. No painting, as a work of art, is ever conceived without pure seeing, which cuts through habit, extraneous ideas, and all other restrictive barriers directly to the thing itself.

This automobile, in *pure* seeing, becomes an oblong black form in relation to other curved forms, with discs on either end. In words, this description sounds cold and not very descriptive. But note that it is not in terms associated with other things. This point is significant. Pure vision is used in painting, a visual medium. Pure vision was also used in designing the car itself. But pure vision cannot be used to describe the car in words; reflective or specialized vision translated into words might do it better, for pure seeing is *purely* visual, and cannot be translated into any other medium.

These differences between pure seeing and other kinds of seeing, I think, are the cause of so much misunderstanding in all art criticism: the attempt to translate pictures into words, a different medium of expression entirely.

Which Picture Do You Like?

HERE ARE FOUR PICTURES to choose from: a baby, some flowers, and two dogs. Try to decide which picture you like the best, and in what order you prefer the other three. Now look at the pictures and make your choice before you read further.

Perhaps your first choice has been the baby, followed by the puppy holding up his paws, the other dog, and then the bowl of flowers. Or flowers may interest you more than dogs, or babies more than flowers, and dogs not at all.

Whatever your preference, how did you arrive at your decision? Did you look at these pictures with specialized, reflective, or pure seeing? Or did you disregard the question entirely, which was about *pictures*, not *things*, and merely express a preference for real babies, as opposed to real dogs or real flowers? And in consequence, did you fail to see the pictures themselves, in addition to their respective subjects?

Photograph by Tatsuo Ishimoto   *Photograph by Tatsuo Ishimoto*

Photography, Painting, and the Human Eye

A PHOTOGRAPH HAS BEEN described as "something to remember something by," a tangible record of a tangible thing. Photographic documentation has long since made naturalistic painting no longer necessary, by supplanting the painter in this field, and freeing him at the same time.

Photography has often imitated painting, and painting has imitated photography, each with a loss of integrity. This basketball photograph, however, is true to its medium, as a picture impossible to duplicate in any other way. Action has been stopped in midair by a precision lens at 1/800 second, and yet such details as highlighted fingernails and the trademark on the ball are sharp and still in focus. A good lens can always "see" much faster than the eye, the result being scientifically of value, but often optically untrue.

The effect of movement in pictures is never the result of accident, such as the freezing of unnatural postures in an instant of time. As observed visually, this action was continuous, a series of rapid and consecutive movements. To see all this with the human eye is virtually impossible, as specific interest always concentrates vision in one place or another, but never in all directions at the same time. The camera, however, is entirely impersonal, and sees everything with equal intensity, in contrast to the selectivity of human vision as seen through the mind.

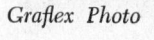
Graflex Photo

The Designed Photograph

WHILE IT IS DIFFICULT to distinguish one photographer's work from another's, it is easily possible to express personal viewpoints in arranging a photograph. But photography is usually at the mercy of things as they are; for no matter what equipment is used, complete control of the subject is seldom possible.

This picture of a window cleaner might be called a designed photograph. But while it has been organized geometrically, the window patterns are still too accidental and would be improved by more variety in accent—impossible to add by photographic means.

In this discussion of photography, painting, and the human eye, accent has been placed on photography's limitations, and very little has been said of the contributions photography has made in scientific research, in medicine, in industry, and in accurately recording all phases of contemporary life. The value of these contributions is well recognized.

RAY BETHERS: Window Cleaner. *From U.S. Camera*

Factual Representation

FACTUAL REPRESENTATION is nothing more than accurate pictorial reporting, the scene being more important than the picture; and aside from being made by hand, it is similar to photography. Realistic painting is not necessarily factual representation, the difference being in degree of emotion and organization in the picture, and not in its surface treatment.

Meissonier's painting, *A General and His Aide-de-Camp,* is an example of factual representation, a catalog of facts relating to the incident but otherwise without pictorial relationships. Any part of this picture can be shifted; some elements may even be removed, the margins trimmed, and still not affect the events illustrated. The picture is no more than a snapshot in paint, accidental in arrangement, monotonous in detail and totally lacking in emotional content. Note how important the shadow in the upper left corner of this picture becomes, in forming a strong diagonal line, pictorially irrelevant, yet calling attention to itself and away from the subject.

The idea of factual representation might be further clarified by a mythical problem in music, a symphonic composition. Let us imagine that a composer is commissioned to write a symphony of fifteen minutes duration, to be called *Times Square.* In carrying out this commission he arrives, with pad and pencil, at Forty-third and Broadway. At exactly 2 p.m. he begins to write, and as each automobile horn is heard, he scores the corresponding notes for French horns; the sounds of pneumatic drills are given to the kettle drums, and violins will imitate a siren's wail. At 2:15 he stops, his composition finished. He has just composed a factual representation covering fifteen minutes of sounds heard in Times Square.

This "composition" would be accurate in some respects, and not exactly the same as though electronically recorded. But it would also be a counterfeit, a total misuse of musical form, without theme, unity, or feeling.

MEISSONIER: A General and his Aide-de-Camp. *Courtesy of the Metropolitan Museum of Art*

The Literary Approach in Pictures

THE STORY-TELLING PICTURE is the most familiar of all phases of *subject* in painting. Many popular magazines have successfully used story-telling pictures for a long time—stories told in pictures that might well have been told in words. This type of picture not only has a subject, but the objects shown are related by participation in a given scene—a static tableau of frozen actors on a two-dimensional stage.

Like factual representation, story telling itself is not at fault; it is the dependence on the story, rather than on emotional organization that limits this type of picture. The painter's effort is entirely directed toward a literary end; costumes, characters, furniture, all correct as related to the story and scene described. Every effort is made to make you *forget* you are looking at a picture, attention being directed to other things— childhood memories, moral precepts, in fact anything except the actual picture.

The picture opposite is a nostalgic anecdote, mellowed somewhat by time. A little girl, on her first trip to the bank, is being encouraged in thrift by a beaming grandma and grandpa. That is the story. If you like the story, you like the picture, and each time you see it, it tells the same story. Similar to "Have you heard this one before—about the little girl who went to the bank . . . ?"

Magazine covers are logical places for story-telling pictures, as their interest is usually limited to the literary story told, and a new picture appears each week.

Like factual painting, literary painting requires great technical skill. the ability to copy *things* in a lifelike and unemotional manner. The parts of the subject being related by literary rather than pictorial means, some parts can even be cut away without the story being affected at all. If any picture *depends* on the story it tells, it is a literary picture, and not a work of art.

Louis C. Moeller, N. A.: Her First Savings. *Courtesy Harry Shaw Newman Gallery, New York City*

Advertising Illustration

ADVERTISING IS A BUSINESS with definite problems of its own, and advertising art should be considered on that basis only, not from a fine-art standpoint. While some advertising illustrations are creative and have emotional content, the very nature of the problem differs materially from the creation of a work of art. Almost every drawing used in advertising has been conceived and composed by people other than the artist who makes the finished drawing; sometimes as many as fifteen persons have influenced the final picture. Aside from all this, restrictions are placed on the artist by printing requirements, by time limitations, by alterations, and by surveys of past public opinion.

Not that advertising couldn't improve on the quality of art work used; but a complicated routine has evolved which is partly to blame, and which could easily be eliminated. First, the advertising conference system has been carried too far, setting up limitations which tie an artist to such an extent that only a small portion of his abilities is ever used. Second, the common advertising conception of realism is mistaken, in the belief that *everything* in a picture must be realistic and of equal emphasis, without selection or unifying design. This demand usually results in pictorial confusion, lack of individuality, and a partial defeat of the advertisement's original aim.

This landscape and train illustration is an example of many restrictions being eliminated at the beginning. This composition was entirely conceived by the artist, and while it is apparently realistic, study will show an organized pattern of related directional lines and forms that attracts attention, eliminates confusion, and encourages visual exploration over a longer period of time.

FRED LUDEKENS: Cascade Route. *Courtesy of the Southern Pacific Railroad*

Photograph used for reference in painting the above picture

Painting to Order

On APRIL 12, 1453, a French artist, Enguerrand Charonton, signed the following contract binding himself to execute a small altarpiece four feet by three. Only a part of the original contract is quoted here.*

"First there shall be the form of Paradise and in this Paradise shall be the Holy Trinity, and between Father and Son shall be no difference; and the Holy Spirit in the form of a dove, and Our Lady, before, as shall seem best to the said Master Enguerrand.

"*Item:* by the side of Our Lady shall be the angel Gabriel with a certain number of angels, and on the other side Saint Michael with such number of angels as shall seem best to the said Master Enguerrand.

"*Item:* on the other hand (the left side) Saint John the Baptist with other patriarchs and prophets according to the judgment of the said Master Enguerrand.

"*Item:* on the right side shall be Saint Peter and Saint Paul with a certain number of other apostles. . . .

"*Item:* shall be in the aforesaid Paradise of every human estate to the ordering of the said Master Enguerrand.

"*Item:* above the said Paradise shall be the heavens in which will be the sun and moon according to the judgment of the said Master Enguerrand. . . .

"*Item:* the said Master Enguerrand shall show all his science in the holy Trinity and the Blessed Virgin and for the rest according to his conscience.

"*Item:* the back of the altarpiece shall be painted with a fine cloth of crimson damask all figured with fleurs de lys."

* Translation from the original French by permission of *The Studio*.

ENGUERRAND CHARONTON: Coronation of the Virgin Mary

The Influence of Photography on Illustration

Emotional content is to be desired in illustration, but it can be shown in ways other than "clinches," the trade name for the boy-girl pictures seen so often in popular magazines. As most of these are drawn directly from photographs, they have little individuality or variety, and aside from the subject, are usually low in emotional content. They are mostly literary, story-telling pictures, an itemized, rather than organized set of facts, and compare pictorially to a story made of words in accidental positions without relation to the total meaning.

Illustration, like advertising art, is made for a specific purpose, and should be considered as a pictorial part of literary expression; as pictures to assist where words fail. And unlike a painting, an illustration is usually incomplete in itself, not only without words, but away from the page for which it was designed.

A good illustration cannot depend entirely on its subject but should add pictorial emotion to the story told. Photographic copying has lately had a serious effect on illustration. Used by illustrators as a substitute for creative drawing, photographs have not only stifled emotion, but have failed to be "realistic" from a purely editorial standpoint.

As an example of *translating* rather than copying from a photograph, this basketball picture has been redesigned from the photograph to approximate movement in an illustrative manner, by the control of relationships and directions. This diagram is not a picture, but only the *structure* of a picture, a diagram of an idea. It is this unifying principle that is missing in many unemotional and static illustrations where photographs have been too much relied upon. Accurate copies of photographic forms will always be impersonal, photographs in everything but time, energy, and paint.

Graflex Photo

Writers on Art

It is not generally realized that almost all the printed pictures we are allowed to see in books, in magazines, or in advertising are chosen by people trained in the use of the written word. So let us examine the writer's viewpoint as regards pictures.

Words, as symbols mutually agreed upon, stand abstractly for some object, action, quality, or the like, and it is usually the writer's job to fit these words to objects, actions, and so on. Now it so happens that painting, being a medium of expression in its own right, as words themselves are, is not always translatable into another medium. It is true that story-telling and factual pictures are not difficult to describe, but a visual work of art, true to its own medium, can only be experienced by direct viewing. Otherwise, why is painting in existence at all?

This fitting of a word to an object seems to cause a pictorial blindness in most writers. They are usually lost without some kind of story, allied to their own trade, fiction or whatever it may be. That tendency, perhaps, accounts for the large percentage of literary pictures selected by literary people to be shown on the printed page. It also causes any purely visual picture to suffer from descriptive writing. A story being absent, it is imagined by the baffled writer, who then adds something that wasn't there. To him, the title is also of great importance, and failing a properly descriptive title, he will add one. It seems that the writer's definition of a picture might be, "something to write a caption for."

It is curious that editors and writers, with their incomplete pictorial viewpoint, should be the filter through which all printed pictures pass. What a queer world it would be if all the writing you read were selected by professional painters in a similar way.

The following is an actual example of the writer's usual approach to pictures. It is taken from an article describing Daumier's water color, *The Third Class Carriage*, a reproduction of this picture having been shown along with the article in question.

I quote in part: "The Third Class is unmistakable. The car is open above the crowded, transverse wooden benches, instead of being divided into compartments, and the passengers are of the solid middle class; businessmen, farmers, and women with shawls and bundles."

Now anyone can see that, just by looking at the picture. Is it necessary to establish the fact that it really is a third-class carriage? Suppose the title had been lost—would the picture still be of consequence?

The writer goes on, comparing this to a similar Daumier: "As he worked, the artist made a few improvements in the composition: the back of the bench was lowered, the bundle beside the boy became a box."

Now that's beginning to talk about the picture. But why did "lowering the back of the bench" improve the composition? It might have weakened it. Does a box make a better composition than a bundle?

Again, speaking of the old woman in the picture: "She sits beside her daughter and grandchildren unmindful of the hard bench and the talk going on around her, thinking over the day just past, and waiting calmly for the end of the journey." This is pure mind-reading—Daumier himself didn't know what the old lady was thinking, and who knows her family relationships? Besides, she is really paint on paper and cannot think at all. Are we not more interested in the way Daumier, as a painter, organized these forms and colors into a work of art: the horizontal line of the bench, the diagonal spotting of the windows, and the pattern of dark coats and hats? Collectively, they are the picture and can only be completely realized by seeing the actual picture. As Daumier himself, once said: "One does not draw a word, one draws a gesture, an expression."

A good critic never attempts to tell you what pictures *you* should like, but rather points out the *type* of painting exhibited, and to what degree he feels it is successful in its own field. He will act as a saver of time and energy, rather than as an arbiter of taste.

HONORÉ DAUMIER: The Third Class Carriage. *Courtesy of the Metropolitan Museum of Art*

[35]

Titles on Works of Art

Should your interests lie both in music and painting, you might doubly enjoy Mussorgsky's *Pictures at an Exhibition*. By the same token, *The 1812 Overture* would be the more understandable to any historian, tone deaf or otherwise. But suppose at a band concert *Anacreon in Heaven* is announced, yet everyone rises as *The Star Spangled Banner* is played, moved by the music rather than by the air's original name. Likewise, titles of works of art seldom lead to greater understanding, any more than knowing a man's name is Henry gives a clue to the character of the man.

It is true that some illustrative and informational pictures need words to complement otherwise incomplete information, but titles of works of art are usually for identification rather than explanation.

This picture by Alexander Brook is a case in point, for it was once used in an advertisement headed "Easing Painful Joints." But it wasn't painted with that idea in mind; its original title was *D-Day*. Which do you think describes the picture better—*Easing Painful Joints* or *D-Day*?

Most painters add titles *after* a picture is finished, their problem being purely pictorial rather than the pictorial interpretation of words. Science may some day eliminate painful joints, and D-Day may pass from living memory, but since many pictures without titles have survived for thousands of years, perhaps some future generation will see this picture for itself, without titles of any kind.

ALEXANDER BROOK: *Courtesy of the Upjohn Company*

The Good Old Days?

OBJECTS BECOME ANTIQUES partly on account of a state of mind—a desire to project the past into present, as seen through rose-colored glasses. This old Currier and Ives lithograph, once new and a part of contemporary life, has now become an antique with all the associations that go with it. Does it bring to mind visions of bad roads, unending toil, or anxious miles in driving for a doctor? Of course not, for those were the good old days, when bad things didn't happen.

But nothing ever happens in the past, good or bad. It has already happened, and with no surprises, new ideas, or new problems; the past is safe and secure, but *no longer possible to live in.*

American Farm Scene. *Currier and Ives Lithograph*

Does History Repeat Itself?

I̲T̲ H̲A̲S̲ N̲O̲T̲ always been so, but the time lag between a painter's work and public appreciation has become about fifty years, as the history of Impressionism will verify. In fact, the public sometimes seems to prefer the work of dead men, as indicated by the policies of certain museums which forbid the purchase of living artists' work. Fortunately this policy has not yet been applied to the work of doctors, lawyers, engineers, and similar professional people.

In 1874, amidst a storm of protest, the Impressionists gave their first exhibition, including, among others, the works of Cézanne, Degas, Monet, Pissarro, and Renoir. Sales were few, and pictures that later sold for enormous sums went for little or not at all. Renoir's painting, *The Dancer*, now in the National Gallery of Art, was shown in this exhibition, and was severely criticised as an example of bad draftmanship. Does it appear badly drawn today?

In succeeding exhibitions, the public and critics alike not only failed to understand these painters, but said so in no uncertain terms. "They take paint, brushes and canvases; they throw a few colors on the canvas at random, and then they sign the lot." The public, attending the exhibition, "laughed as they were going up the stairs; they were convulsed with laughter the first moment they cast their eyes upon the pictures." If that were not enough, another critic wrote, "They display the profoundest ignorance of drawing, of composition, and of color. When children amuse themselves with a box of colors and a piece of paper they do better." *

This last line must sound familiar; perhaps it wasn't new, even then.

* *Cubists and Post-Impressionism*, by Arthur Jerome Eddy. Chicago, A. C. McClurg & Co., 1919.

PIERRE AUGUSTE RENOIR: The Dancer. *National Gallery of Art, Washington, D.C.; Widener Collection*

Awards: the Jury versus the People

It would seem that a competent jury of artists, critics, and museum directors should know in advance what the public would like, and the fact is, they usually do. Almost all the public's awards have been given to story-telling (literary) pictures or to familiar factual representations of nature, the accent having so far been on "what" it is rather than on "how" it is done. These same subjects have been winners time after time, as museums, advertising agencies, popular magazines, and Hollywood well know. However, if pictures were chosen on the basis of total popularity, the comic sections would win with no trouble at all.

But museums have other standards which are usually reflected in a jury's point of view. Paintings are seldom judged by subject, story-telling, or "timely" qualities; the jury aims instead to present pictures that in their judgment will endure, without an extraneous literary or factual crutch to lean on.

The two pictures shown here are both prize winners. Frederick J. Waugh's painting, *March—North Atlantic,* has been exhibited extensively throughout the United States. Where a public poll was taken, "the Waugh has been a two-to-one favorite of the public." Why is this?

It is first of all a familiar subject, a well-executed seascape, and in its way a "copy of nature." It looks real, almost photographic, and people find the picture easy to understand. But how different it is in all respects from Karl Knaths' painting, *Gear,* which won the jury first prize in one of our most important exhibitions, Carnegie's "Painting in the United States, 1946." This picture makes no attempt at realism; it is a designed picture, and does not depend on its subject for justification.

The test of popularity in art is, finally, not how many people like a picture today but how many people will like a picture over a long period of time.

FREDERICK J. WAUGH: March—North Atlantic. *Copyright Encyclopaedia Britannica, Inc.; from the Encyclopaedia Britannica Collection of Contemporary American Painting*

KARL KNATHS: Gear. *Winner of First Prize, Carnegie's "Painting in the United States, 1946"; photograph courtesy Paul Rosenberg & Co.*

[43]

Propaganda in Art

WHEN A PICTURE attempts to change a condition—a wrong (or right)—which the painter feels strongly about, that is a propaganda picture, but not necessarily art. A painter's emotional state can sometimes lead to overemphasis on subject with corresponding structural neglect. Any subject which stirs a painter's emotions is good, as far as the artist himself is concerned, but there is no guarantee that great work will result from that emotion. Too much emotion can be as bad as not enough.

William Gropper's *The Senate,* as a propaganda picture, can be considered a success, but is this success brought about by its subject or by the design of the picture? A propaganda picture, as a work of art, should continue to be emotionally stirring, even though the condition it set out to change has long since passed away. Or should the title be lost, or the observer know nothing of its original intent, the picture as a work of art should not lose in consequence. Otherwise, it becomes of historical value only, with no place any longer in a museum of art.

WILLIAM GROPPER: The Senate. *Collection of the Museum of Modern Art, New York*

Historical Pictures

IF ANY PICTURE, historic or otherwise, depends entirely on its subject, it may have great documentary value but very little value as a work of art. On the other hand, a work of art may have secondary subject interest such as history, and be unaffected from an art standpoint even though historically incorrect in detail.

For many years this historic picture, *Washington Crossing the Delaware,* has appeared in schoolbooks, illustrating how General Washington and his men crossed this river during the Revolutionary War. The artist, Emanuel Leutze, was a German and used German soldiers as models when he painted the picture in Düsseldorf, in 1851. But this is relatively unimportant, as compared to the picture's many errors in historic fact. In the first place, the flag as shown was designed later, and was not in existence in 1776. The crossing actually took place under cover of darkness, as part of the strategy, but this fact is not shown in the picture. And in addition, historical records describe how General Washington "sat in silence on a beehive" during the passage.

In other words, the picture is not historic, and *does not* show how Washington crossed the Delaware. How, then, shall it be regarded?

EMANUEL LEUTZE: Washington Crossing the Delaware. *Courtesy of the Metropolitan Museum of Art*

Portraits

WHAT IS A PORTRAIT? Should it look precisely like the subject, be an unimaginative factual representation, or be an artist's interpretation, combining the artist's viewpoint with the character of the subject? Should a good portrait not only have personal interest to the subject and his immediate family, but be of interest as a work of art to the general public as well?

The three portrait paintings shown here are part of an experiment carried out by Abraham Walkowitz, a painter himself, in having his portrait painted by one hundred artists over a year's time. The total result is of great interest, as Mr. Walkowitz says, "Each artist saw himself as he painted, in addition to portraying the character of the subject."

Photograph of Abraham Walkowitz

Moise Kisling

Joe Jones

Louis Ribak

Dictionary of Terms

ABSTRACT: This word has been used in various ways in relation to art, and needs clarification. As used here, it *does not* mean *abstracted from* nature.

The Museum of Modern Art, New York, in *Cubism and Abstract Art*, says: "'Abstract' is the term most frequently used to describe the more extreme effect of the impulse *away* from 'nature'." In other words, as a picture gets further from "nature," it becomes more abstract, becoming, by degrees, a "near abstraction," and when all relation to the world of actuality is gone, it is called a "pure abstraction." Pictures described by this term "pure abstraction" are also known as "concrete," or "non-objective." But while it is important to understand terms, it is much more important to recognize the quality described by the term in an actual picture.

PLANE: A plane is usually not seen, in itself, but gives the felt direction and relationships of forms in pictorial space.

PICTURE PLANE: The flat surface of the picture itself.

FORMAT: The proportion of the picture plane. Format can also refer to size.

SPACE: Pictorial space does not actually exist, but is achieved by various means such as overlapping planes, certain uses of diagonal lines, perspective, and other devices. *Limited* space means that the eye is not carried to unlimited depth into a picture, in terms of apparent space.

PERSPECTIVE: A mechanical system of imitating the effect of forms as they recede in space.

TEXTURE: This may be an actual texture, rough or smooth, on the surface of the picture, or a texture may be indicated by spots, lines, or other methods of breaking an otherwise plain surface.

LINE: A line can be just a line, but the word is sometimes used to denote the collective movement and direction of several lines or forms.

PATTERN: Pattern is two-dimensional, elements lying flat on the picture plane, with no indication of space. Pattern can be pleasing to the eye, but it evokes no such great depth of feeling as is possible in three-dimensional painting.

[50]

VOLUME: Form with thickness. A cube, as a volume in space, can be tilted or turned to any position, and lie on any plane. Even volumes of no particular relation to geometric shapes are sometimes thought of as cubic forms, in establishing the particular volume in space.

BALANCE: Not necessarily symmetry, but relationships of forms, lines, textures, elements, which collectively balance one another in a picture.

VALUE: The relationship of a color to a scale of grays graduated from black to white. Yellow is a light value, purple a dark value.

NEGATIVE SPACE: The space surrounding positive forms in space. A bottle shown in a picture would be positive, the surrounding space, negative.

TWO-DIMENSIONAL: Flat, as a picture plane is flat.

THREE-DIMENSIONAL: The effect of space in painting—length, height, and depth. A picture can have two-dimensional and three-dimensional qualities, both at the same time—the two-dimensional pattern on the picture plane may also be organized in relation to the idea of space.

Art Is Not a Copy of Nature (I)

Art is always made by a man, for men, which is, of course, not a characteristic of nature. Art complements nature, perhaps, but the emotion derived from the two is different, so rather than expect art to be a copy of nature, why not accept the two as different and enjoy both?

In a geographic informational sense, a picture can be useful which shows a certain place and time, but would still be only an imitation of nature, and could never take nature's place. It is characteristic of pictures to be flat, confined to certain areas, and created by man's hand, brain, and innermost feelings—and although effects of nature have inspired many painters, an artist never tries to copy nature; he adds his own creative feelings to any inspiration he may have received.

The Impressionists, notably Claude Monet, tried to copy certain aspects of nature, chiefly the effect of light on natural forms. By painting in primary colors, broken into small strokes, a remarkable simulation of sunlight was achieved, but the results were usually more scientific than otherwise. In this search for scientific accuracy, Monet painted the same scene, *Haystacks,* under varying atmospheric conditions, changing canvases from hour to hour to follow the continual variations.

But in concentrating on *one* of nature's phases, Monet failed both to add his personal feeling, and to organize his forms in relation to the picture as a work of art.

CLAUDE MONET: Haystacks. *Courtesy of the Metropolitan Museum of Art*

Let's Paint a Picture (in Words)

Me: It's sunny; a very pleasant day here in the country. Why not sit down while I paint a picture, and ask me all the questions you like?

You: Thanks, I always did like loafing while other people work. What are you going to paint?

Me: As I came along the road, that white house against the red barn, with the cattle in the foreground, interested me.

You: Do you like cattle?

Me: No, just the color of the cattle. Now I'll start washing in color as quickly as possible, just the main areas of the picture first, in order to cover the white of the canvas.

You: That surprises me, I thought you'd start at the top and work your way down.

Me: No. It's best to work all over the picture at once, for everything you do affects everything else. And, besides, it's difficult to judge color accurately on a pure white surface; white, the house, for instance, will look whiter as shown against the red of the barn.

You: Then why do you paint the house light yellow? It looks white to me.

Me: That's a painter's device, a method to approximate the warmth of sunlight, for I'm painting with paint, which is very limited compared to the range of actual light.

You: I don't see any tree where you just drew that one!

Me: I don't either, but your eye would go right out of the picture at that point, if I didn't put something there to keep your interest *within* the picture. You see, a picture is only a small section of the landscape, and while you stand here in the out-of-doors, you can look in any and all directions. But the picture must seem complete in itself when it's finished, rather than be just a fragment of everything you can see from here.

You: That's an odd way to paint grass. You're making it red, but it certainly looks green to me.

Me: Colors have a kind of magic in themselves, and affect one another in strange ways. I am painting the grass red, but in a moment, I'll paint green loosely over the red, letting some of the red show through. This will produce a vibration, a *new* color effect impossible to get in any other way.

You: Now, I see you're moving the cows around. Is that to keep my eye in the picture, too?

Me: Yes and no. I'm making a pattern of the cows, in relation to the barn and trees. In painting, the way the artist feels towards his composition is more important than where cows may accidentally be, at any particular time. But after all, the cows can also change their own position.

You: Well, perhaps they do look better that way. Just like rearranging furniture can sometimes give a better effect. But why did you make the top of that roof darker just now? I see it the same color all over.

Me: That's an accent, like accenting a word in conversation. The roof would be monotonous without it, and it's part of the general movement.

You: I don't see any movement!

Me: Well, the movement doesn't actually move. I mean a sort of eye track, a relationship of spots, lines, and spaces, which leads you to explore the entire picture in an orderly fashion. The addition of that extra tree was also part of this unifying idea.

You: You know, all this time I thought you were trying to copy nature, and now it looks as though you're trying to improve on nature.

Me: No, I'm just trying to paint a picture, not copy nature. Why not enjoy nature and painting, too, as a sort of double feature? Painting can't *be* nature anyway; it's made by man, for men, and its emotional appeal is very different from that of nature.

You: But I like color photographs!

Me: So do I. But don't get them confused with a work of art. They may look like nature, but they aren't nature either. They are a kind of pictorial information, like reporting.

You: What's wrong with information?

Me: Nothing, but do you want information all the time?

You: I thought *I* was the one to *ask* questions!

Me: So you are, but coming back to your other question, I take certain information from nature when I paint, and use it as material for my picture, which is another thing, entirely.

You: You paint very fast. I'm wondering, do you *think* every time you add a brush stroke to the picture?

Me: Didn't Shakespeare ask, "Tell me where is fancy bred, in the heart or in the head?" Yes, I do think, and no, I don't. Part is thinking, of course, but suddenly instinct will take charge and do the painting for me.

You: If I asked another artist all these questions, would I get the same answers?

Me: Would you like the same answers?

You: I do like to know where I stand!

Me: Well, it's something like this: if one artist creates a work of art, and someone else makes one exactly like it, the second one is bound to be a copy and not a work of art. So, you can't measure one artist against another; you can only like one better. Someone else may disagree entirely with your choice, and still be right, but only as far as he, himself, is concerned. It's just like shopping; we don't all shop in the same kind of places, we go to different shops for different things.

You: Do you get upset when people say, "I don't know anything about art, but I know what I like"?

Me: Of course not. That's a very true statement, even if it has been overworked. *You* are the one who does the liking, so you should know what you like. Paintings that you don't understand, you simply don't "see." What people really mean is that they like what they know; for most anyone feels lost in unfamiliar surroundings.

You: But how do I know, when I look at a picture, that I'm really seeing it?

Me: You'll know!

You: I always like pictures of boats.

Me: All pictures of boats, good, bad, and indifferent?

You: Well, I like the sails to be correct.

Me: That's information again, and besides, it's information you already know.

You: I had an uncle once, who painted wonderful pictures of deer, and he never had a lesson in his life.

Me: Lots of people paint pictures who never had a lesson. It's the picture that matters, not the deer, or boats either. Pictures, if they're works of art, will give you an inner satisfaction, an emotion which has nothing to do with deer, boats, or any other subject. Some pictures of objects have no more emotional quality than the telephone book.

You: Well, I may not know much about pictures, but I do like listening to music.

Me: Why not try looking at a work of art in the same way you listen to music, without trying to identify things, or to find a story. Just enjoy it for itself, and what it does *to* you, not for you.

You: Now that you've finished your sketch, is it a work of art?

Me: Only *you* can know that. So what does it say to you?

You: It's nice, but doesn't look much like the place you painted it from.

Me: Perhaps you'll like it better in a frame.

Emotion and the Artist

ART IS ALWAYS the product of *both* emotion and thought—not entirely emotion, for a purely emotional state is unstable and will interfere with any kind of creative effort. Ever since *Trilby* and *La Bohème*, the popular conception of an artist has been one of long hair, flowing tie, and "artistic" temperament. But while an artist does have temperament, it is usually expressed in sensitivity rather than in idiosyncrasies of behavior and dress.

Emotion is a very important part of the painting process, but has been generally misunderstood. A painter's emotion is instinctive; he *sometimes* paints without effort, ideas developing without apparent reason, but at other times reason is uppermost and pictorial problems are solved with almost mathematical precision.

Can you imagine a painter, working for months on a sad picture, with continual tears blinding his efforts? He is no more directly affected than an actor, gay in one scene and tragic in the next, is personally concerned with the emotions of the character he portrays. The artist's aim is to produce emotion in the observer, rather than to go through the same emotion himself.

Music

ALL ARTS have two things in common: they never tell the whole story, and are always incomplete without *your* participation. When several art forms are combined, as in sound motion pictures, the sum total is apparently more real and less is left to the imagination. And when three-dimensional color and sound motion pictures come into general use, they will appear still more *real*, leave still less to the imagination, and far *more* people will be able to enjoy them *less*. In other words, you receive in direct proportion to what you have to give, in any form of art appreciation.

Music is totally without subject, and consequently allows a higher degree of participation, more so alone than in combination with other forms—words, for instance. Is it not sometimes more enjoyable to hear a song in a foreign language, without knowing the subject of the song?

Perhaps the earliest musical form was rhythm alone, without changes of pitch, as an accompaniment to tribal dancing. A scale was a later and further complication, as were chords and other devices, all developing finally into modern symphonic orchestration with its countless notes on a great variety of instruments.

All music *is* complex, but simple at the same time, and is composed somewhat like a pictorial work of art. No matter how complex the orchestration may be, it is always unified by a central theme, and as in painting this unifying design is related to mathematics. In the case of music, notes are rhythmically arranged on a string of time, depending for their effect on memory of the notes already played and the realization of notes still to come. In painting, forms are organized on an area in space, seen simultaneously, and in most works of art geometrically organized. This unity is felt rather than consciously seen, but all forms of art must have some unifying element to integrate the parts into a satisfying whole.

The Stage

THE STAGE IS "let's pretend," a land of make believe, and still another opportunity for your participation. We do not demand a "copy of nature" here, but go prepared to accept certain devices of the theater, many unrealistic but for that very reason adding to our pleasure. Like a painting, a play is confined to a certain area, the proscenium comparing to a picture's frame. All action is necessarily restricted to this space, which limits the action but also intensifies it. Even the device of speaking aside, or to the audience directly, is not taken from real life but is a convention, and is accepted without question as part of the *play*.

Glenn Wessels uses the following story for comparing real life to that of the theater, and in addition, for describing the detached way to look at painting as a fine art. He says: "Imagine you are in the audience, a spectator and personally detached from the action taking place on the stage. A shot is fired, a man is murdered in the play. This you accept as imaginary, and feel no compulsion to actively enter into this situation.

"Everything has so far taken place in the realm of imagination, but suddenly a man runs down the aisle, draws a pistol, and shoots an unknown woman at your side. Now you *are* shocked; no longer passive, you spring to action at once. Then you discover you've been fooled, that this bit of 'realism' is part of the play after all, and personal action is not required.

"But you have received an actual shock. A false and *realistic* intrusion has rudely taken you out of the realm of detachment, of art, and back into the world of reality."

Art Doesn't Change

ART DOESN'T CHANGE; it is never old, and is never new. It may sometimes appear to change, but this change will be only on the surface; for all art is timeless, far beyond historic, racial, or geographic influence. A work of art, newly finished, is a new thing in the world, and may speak what appears to be a new language, but essentially it springs from the same source as all other works of art, and can be emotionally experienced in exactly the same way.

Art and science have sometimes been compared, but they have very little in common. Art, while not changing, differs from science in a great many ways: art answers fundamental human needs, both intellectual and emotional, while science supplies only physical requirements. Science, however, does change; new things are continually being discovered, but unfortunately far faster than the human race has so far been able to absorb them.

Mario Carreño: Diana—1946. *Courtesy Perls Galleries*

Luca Cambiaso (1527-1585): *Men Wrestling or Fighting. Collection Uffizi, Florence*

Reindeer. Painted by Cave Men about 20,000 Years Ago. *Photograph courtesy of the American Museum of Natural History*

Art Is a Road

ART IS A ROAD, an endless road of adventures of the spirit. And all roads are different, as many as there are people to follow them.

To begin the journey, don't insist on factual representation, the photographic approach. Did you ever see a photograph of an idea? To say, "But it doesn't look natural," is to put blinders on yourself; art is always a personal experience, and *not* a copy of nature.

And don't look for literary stories in pictures, for most paintings, as works of art, tell an entirely different kind of story. Hidden behind the subject can be what might be called "visual music," a pictorial story that can't be told in words.

So give pictures a chance to speak. Many, but not all, will have something to say to *you*.

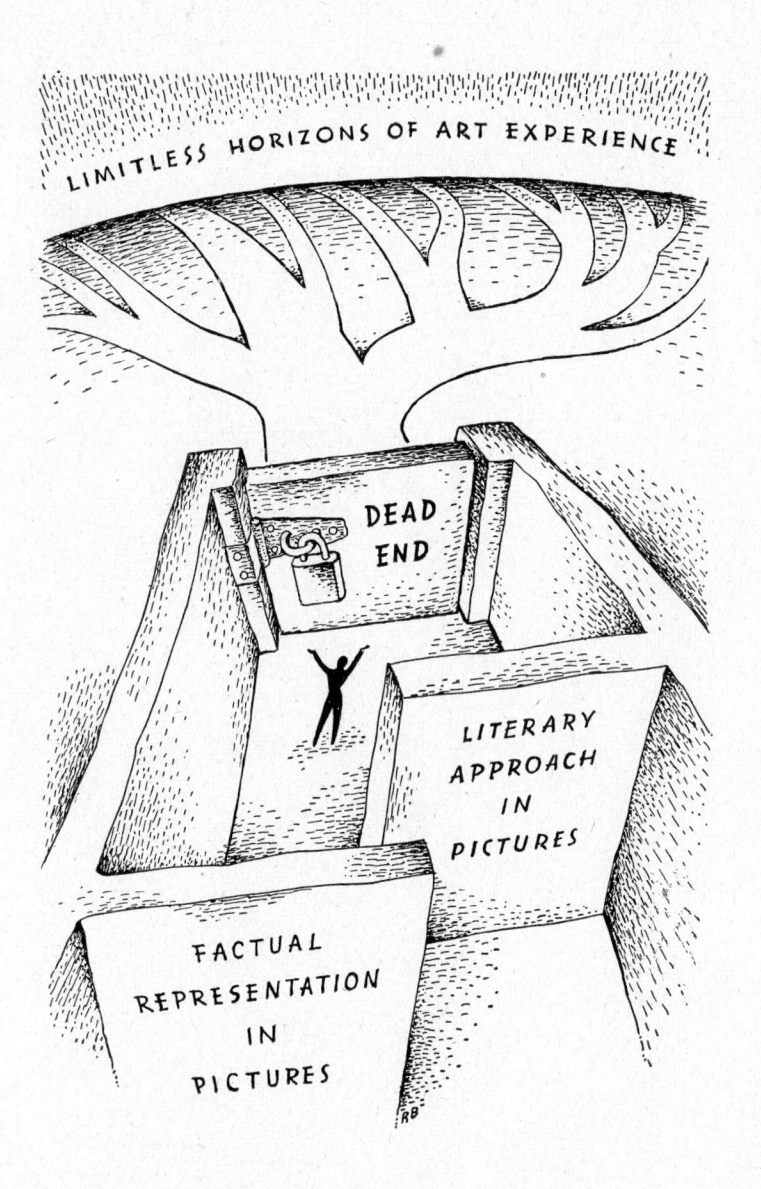

LIMITLESS HORIZONS OF ART EXPERIENCE

DEAD END

LITERARY APPROACH IN PICTURES

FACTUAL REPRESENTATION IN PICTURES

How Real Is Real?

Look carefully for a moment. Does this man's head appear *real* to you? If so, perhaps you have already accepted many abstract ideas not before realized.

Below is a partial list of "devices," all untrue to nature, but incorporated here, and necessary to express this simple pictorial idea.

1. *Flat Surface.* A real head has three dimensions. This one only appears so, being drawn on an absolutely flat surface.

2. *Line.* There are no lines in nature. A line is simply an idea, used to convey other ideas.

3. *Color.* Nature always appears in color. This drawing has none of the color seen in the actual world.

4. *Size.* The disparity in size with an actual head is readily apparent.

5. *Light and Shade.* No light source is indicated; there is no light and shade in the drawing. Form is indicated in other ways.

6. *Black and White.* Not only are the colors of nature missing, but this effect is produced entirely by *black* in relation to the *white* area of the paper.

Following the Road

THE DIRECTION YOU TRAVEL will always be of your own choosing, and the discoveries you make will always be your own. But there are many paths to follow, and the chart shown on the two following pages points out only one broad and general direction, from realism to abstraction. It might be called the path of abstraction in pictures.

The word *abstraction*, as used here, means degree *away* from nature, and not abstracted from it. Hence the chart begins with the accidental realism of the subject, a church (not used in the chart as a photograph, but as the church itself), then through increasing degrees of abstraction to complete lack of subject, to abstraction in its purest form. Please bear in mind that these pictures are diagrams, not works of art, and are used merely to help clarify the idea of abstraction.

In the first place, the chart follows the general plan of this book—from realism to abstraction—and also parallels the development, over a period of time, of many artists and others who appreciate art. In addition, most pictures can be compared, in degree of abstraction, to some position on the chart.

While varying degrees of abstraction are shown, they are all arbitrary, and could have been done in many different ways. Pure abstraction logically belongs at the extreme end, yet it is somewhat different from the others and is usually conceived without reference to objects in the actual world. And, while the chart shows progressive abstraction, it is intended to show a direction rather than to indicate one degree as better than another. To be of value, this chart should be interpreted only in a broad and general way.

1. *Subject;* complete emphasis on subject without personal point of view. Forms and spaces, light and shade, all in the accidental relationships of the actual world.

2. *Subject simplified,* but forms and spaces, light and shade still pictorially unrelated. A collection of useful facts, but otherwise pictorially uninteresting.

5. *More abstract* than the preceding, it is essentially the same in drawing, but elements have been simplified; the pattern overlaying picture has changed.

6. *Transparency;* pattern and space are more evident as church parallels picture plane, triangular space pattern penetrates through church. Based on horizontal, vertical, diagonal.

[66]

3. *Arranged,* to some extent, by centering the church, shifting trees and placing clouds in the sky, figure added for human interest. An illustrative picture.

4. *Unified* to the picture's format, with a scheme of opposing diagonals to organize forms, to bring the church, road, hills, trees, and figures into closer pictorial relationship.

7. *Near abstraction,* still has pattern and space, but subject almost entirely disappears, due to removal of descriptive steeple, windows, and figures.

8. *Pure abstraction,* without space or subject. Pure abstraction would not necessarily be developed in the foregoing steps, but could be composed without reference to the actual world.

[67]

The Nude

A NUDE IN A PICTURE is quite different from an actual nude; a picture is visual, and no matter what its subject, cannot be a substitute for objects in the actual world.

Here are three pictures of the nude which form a short outline of progressive abstraction. All are similar in subject, but differ in other ways. The figure in the photograph, for instance, shows only an individual at a certain place and time. Pictorial relationships are accidental, unrelated, and uncontrolled.

The Degas painting, though similar in subject, is carefully designed. Every element in the picture is a part, not only of the subject, but of the picture also. Notice how the figure forms an arrangement of verticals and horizontals, leading from the lower left, up to and including the figure of the maid on the right. The robe creates flowing lines in the same direction, and opposing this movement is the diagonal line of the couch which restores the picture's balance. If this arrangement is not evident, turn the picture upside down and it will be more readily seen.

André Lhote has gone a step further, and in this case the *picture* has become much more important than the subject.

This picture will be called "out of drawing" by some, and it is if photography is taken as a guide. But the picture was intended to give visual satisfaction from itself, from its sensitive and integrated design, rather than to describe a particular person at a particular time.

If information from the actual world is expected from this type of painting, then the mistake is yours, for if looked at in this way the picture will be forever misunderstood.

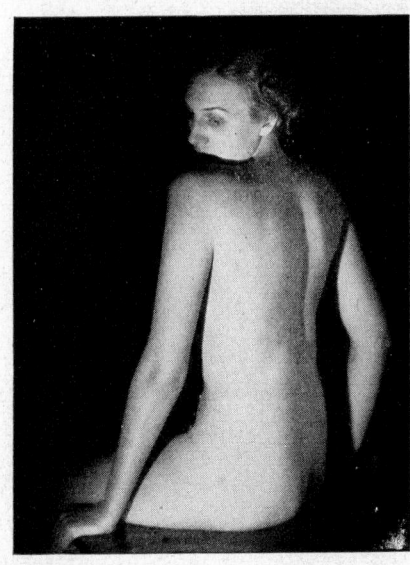

Photograph, copyright Underwood and Underwood

Edgar Degas: The Toilet. *Courtesy of the Metropolitan Museum of Art*

André Lhote: Nude

[69]

Evolution of Pictures

"THE ARTIST HAS AN IDEA for a picture which he puts on canvas exactly as seen in his mind's eye." That seems to be the general impression of the way a painter works, but the process isn't usually so simple. The idea is liable to be vague at first, unformed, and only strong enough to stimulate a picture's beginning.

The first line in a composition may turn out to be very important in influencing other lines and spaces. Instinct will also play a large part as a picture develops, and what seemed just right at an earlier stage may be eliminated later, the picture being continually subject to change. Not only may the design elements change, but sometimes even the subject, in relation to the *pictorial* problem.

In the progressive pictures shown on the following pages, note how Matisse alters his painting as it goes along. At the beginning it is close to observed reality—to the thing itself—but is continually adjusted and shifted towards a purely pictorial end, in a desire to produce a work of art, rather than a copy of something already in existence. Note how long the same light background persisted during the process, to be eliminated at the very end.

In the Picasso lithographs, which come after Matisse, the development is very similar. All eight of these pictures are pulled from the same lithographic stone.

Feb. 26, 1937

March 3, 1937

March 23, 1937

March 24, 1937

March 12, 1937

March 22, 1937

April 3, 1937

The Finished Painting

HENRI MATISSE: The Blue Dress. *Courtesy of the Magazine of Art*

[73]

1

3

2

4

Sequence continues on following pages.

5

7

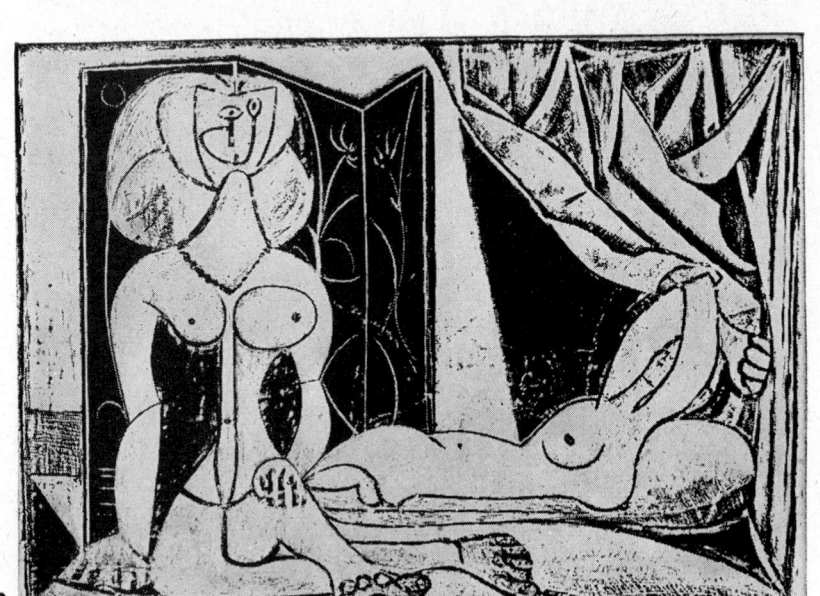

6

8

PABLO PICASSO: Two Figures. Lithograph. *From the
Collection of Mrs. Meric Callery. Photographs courtesy
of the Museum of Modern Art, New York*

WASSILY KANDINSKY: *Tunisian Sheep Festival*—1904. *Museum of Non-Objective Painting, New York*

From Realism to Abstraction* (in Time)

IN THESE THREE PAINTINGS, by Kandinsky, painted over a period of about thirty years, is demonstrated his gradual departure from dependence on subject matter to pictures without relation to the actual world. These pictures not only show the path followed by Kandinsky, but also indicate the general direction many other painters and appreciators of painting have traveled over a period of time.

---

* Wassily Kandinsky preferred to call his later paintings "concrete," or "non-objective," rather than "abstract."

Wassily Kandinsky: Landscape—1910. *Museum of Non-Objective Painting, New York*

Wassily Kandinsky: Supplemented Brown—1935. *Museum of Non-Objective Painting, New York*

[79]

Order, Balance, Rhythm, and Geometry

Our CITIES, HOUSES, rooms and furniture are essentially geometric, as compared to the freer forms in nature. Almost all of our actions are toward order in some way; flowers are planted in mathematical sequence, buttons are evenly spaced, and even music and poetry are indirectly forms of mathematical expression.

This geometric quality seems to be inherent in the human race, even a line of chorus girls becomes a disorganized mob without the rhythmic (and geometric) subordination of the individual to the movement as a whole. A feeling for balance is also instinctive; who can resist moving a lamp to the center of a table if it stands too near the edge?

Any piece of furniture, slightly off-angle from the wall, becomes immediately apparent, and demands attention. It is this kind of instinct that underlies pictorial composition, instinctive with the painter and the observer as well. It is fundamental to react to relationships, of one thing to another. In the diagram shown below, notice how the *odd*, the out-of-relation square is immediately apparent in both cases.

It is this fact of optical relationships which gives variety to painting. The way lines, shapes, and directions are related to one another and to the area where they appear is very similar to relationships in music, where some notes are "compared" with others in pitch, volume, and time. But while order is a fundamental to all forms of art, order itself is monotonous; the ultimate balance will be found in *order* combined by *emotion* with *variety*.

[80]

The Radio City Music Hall Rockettes, world-celebrated precision dancers

Light and Shade

No ARTIST USES LIGHT and shade as found in nature; any painter who allowed nature to dictate to such an extent would find it impossible to do creative work.

This photograph is an example of form destroyed by accidental light and shade. In fact, this same principle is the basis of camouflage, where it is called "disruptive pattern." An artist could use light and shadows to paint a subject similar to the photograph, but his light and shade would be controlled, and would accent the form rather than destroy it.

In William Gropper's painting *The Hunt*, light and shade as seen in nature are not present at all. Note the sensitive handling of *lights* and *darks* instead, related to the picture rather than to the light and shade of the actual world. The trees on the left have become a lacy pattern in pure silhouette, without shadows, and are light against dark instead. There is an interweaving of dark patterns against light, and light against dark, throughout the picture. The dogs are primarily pattern, again without shadow, and are more clearly seen in relation to the picture, in consequence. The entire picture is united by a somewhat oval series of light shapes, rotating from foreground into background. Other relationships will also be found moving throughout this picture.

Other painters may approach this problem differently, but light and shade in nature ordinarily have very little in common with light and shade as used in art.

Natural light and shade as it destroys form

WILLIAM GROPPER: The Hunt. *Courtesy of the Metropolitan Museum of Art*

Darks for Unification

THE DARK ELEMENTS of a picture have a great influence in the design of most compositions, and, in a work of art, are placed by the artist in relation to the picture rather than in their momentary or accidental locations in nature.

In diagram 1, three houses, without volume, are symmetrically balanced on the picture plane. This arrangement produces a simple pattern, but the effect is monotonous and lacking in variety.

In diagram 2, variety and space have been added; variety in placing, and space by relationship to the picture plane and by overlapping planes.

Diagram 3 shows a naturalistic interpretation of light and shade on these forms, somewhat as they would appear in the actual world. This approach throws the *picture* out of balance, and does not adequately explain the form.

In diagram 4, the dark pattern has been considered as a unifying element in the picture, and arbitrarily placed for that reason only. In this case, the artist controls the form and its relation to the picture, rather than being at the mercy of shadows resulting from the sun's position.

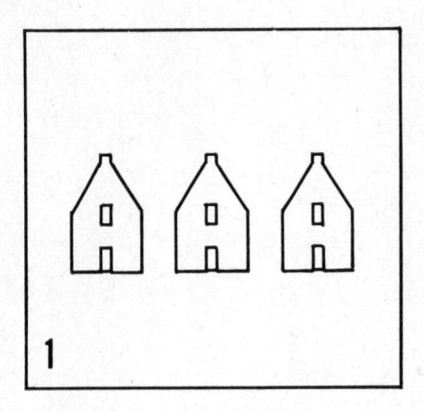

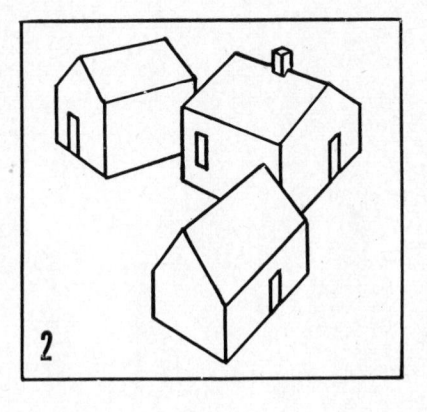

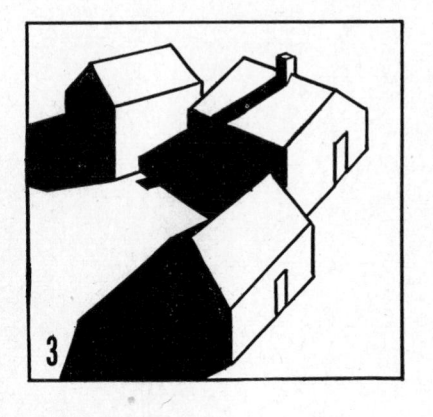

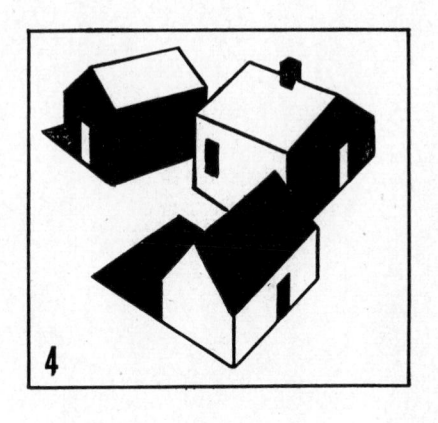

Color and Value

ALL THE PICTURES reproduced in this book are shown in *value*—that is, in their black, white, and gray relation to the color in the actual picture. It would be preferable, but impossible, to show all pictures in full color; but for the most part, pictures are organized from a *dark* and *light* standpoint, relying on the *value* of the particular color.

Color is a science, as far as mixing, etc., is concerned. The use of color as an art begins with relationships of color on an area, combined with relationships of size, texture, value, hue, and intensity. There are *no new colors*, only confusing new names for colors: for example, "the new colors for spring, cactus green, desert gray," and so on.

The three basic qualities of all color are value, hue, and intensity.

Value concerns the relation of a color to dark or light. Yellow is a light value, purple is dark.

Hue is the color of the color, at its purest: red, blue, yellow, etc.

Intensity is the strength. Pure red would be red's highest intensity. A very light pink, made by adding white to red, would still be a derivative of red, but at low intensity. Mixtures, as in a grayed red and yellow (which might be called a brown) are also of low intensity. Colors are *tints* when they approach white, *shades* when they approach black. Grayed color can either be a tint or a shade.

White is not a prismatic color, but is considered to represent all color, as black (also not a color) is a complete absence of color.

This chart demonstrates how the same middle gray value (without color) can be made to appear as a dark (against white) or as a light (against black). This scientific fact, which allows great value variety in pictorial composition, is much more complex when extended into full color relationships.

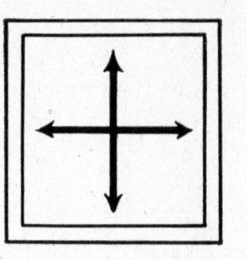

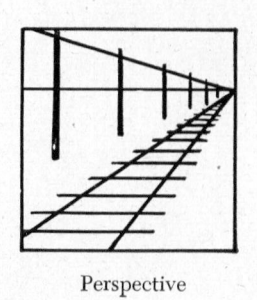

The Picture Plane   Pictorial Space   Perspective

The Picture Plane and the Idea of Space

A WORK OF ART is painted on a *flat* surface, and while objects may appear to have volume, they will be kept behind the actual picture plane. Note the unpleasant illusion, in the picture shown opposite, of the lectern which appears to break the picture plane. While not breaking the picture plane, by thrusting outward, a work of art does give the idea of space, usually limited in depth, and as the eye is taken back into the picture some means is usually employed for a return to the picture plane.

The central diagram, an "exploded cube," illustrates how space can be shown in pictures, by forms overlapping in relation to one another, *behind* the picture plane. This method is in contrast to the use of perspective, which, as shown in the diagram, is inclined to lead the eye *out* of the picture and to offer no means of return.

In a picture seen from above, planes will overlap from front to back in space (as in the actual world); and if we transfer this to the picture plane, the lowest point will be *forward*, the top of the picture plane *back*. This transfer is demonstrated by the overlapping planes in the "picture box" opposite, the space moving from lower left to upper right.

The idea of pictorial space is a "device," related to picture making, and failure to employ it in painting, as in "copying nature," will only result in a confused picture. However, many other elements—pattern, dark and light arrangement, line directions, and the like—also enter into the idea of pictorial space.

Lectern, open bookcase, etc., inlaid in wood as
part of an actual wall. *Courtesy of the Metropolitan Museum of Art*

The Idea of Planes

PLANES ARE PART of the construction of a picture, usually felt rather than actually seen. Planes help to establish positions and directions in space; planes tip, turn, lie flat, or take various positions, and in consequence give conviction to the entire composition.

In this diagram, the larger planes in the painting *Sunday* are indicated. As can be seen, planes 1, 2, 5, 6 and 7 are vertical, but turned away from the picture plane. Plane 3 lies flat, at an angle, as a receding plane and establishes a base for most of the other planes. Plane 4 is both tilted and turned, at an angle to the picture plane. Plane 8 is not tilted or turned, but is parallel to the picture plane.

Forms, or parts of forms, are said to "lie on" a particular plane, as shown by the windows on plane 1.

Note how the overlapping of planes gives a feeling of space, as they recede into the background of the picture. The crossed arrows on each plane in the diagram help to establish the plane's direction, in relation to the picture plane.

Tensions, or relationships, are set up between planes, as indicated by the heavy black arrow between planes 5 and 6, which add to this spatial feeling.

Even the back, unseen planes—the far side of the church, for instance, affect pictorial space and movement. There is even a strong relationship (or tension) between planes as far apart as 1 and 7 in this diagram.

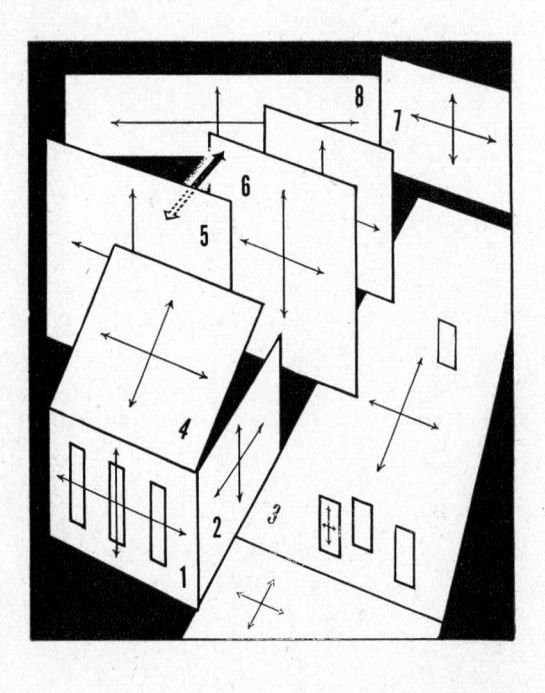

RAY BETHERS: Sunday

The Iron Hand of Perspective

COUNTLESS WORKS OF ART were created long before the Fifteenth Century, when mechanical perspective was invented, Paolo Uccello being usually credited with developing the formula as we know it today.

Architects, engineers, and mechanical draftsmen find perspective a time-saving device, but for the creative painter it forces composition into channels not of the artist's making.

In perspective, once vanishing points are established, every additional line must fall into a preordained position. For example, here is a short quote from a standard textbook on the subject: "Rule a horizontal base line touching the near corner of the picture plane, and another at P. Rule the line of sight perpendicular to these from P, and mark the P.V.P." It is a mechanical system, a limitation without freedom of choice.

It is true that parallel lines, as seen in nature, do appear to converge. But in perspective, they converge much too fast, contrary to the evidence of our own two eyes. Having *two* eyes, we see partially around all objects, getting a feeling of volume in space, the "roundness of things," a quality possible to achieve in art, but not by perspective. A knowledge of perspective is useful for a painter, however, if he doesn't permit this knowledge to control the design elements of his pictures.

The painting shown opposite is purposely not drawn in correct perspective. In perspective, the horizon is *always* on a level with the eyes of the painter. The road and church, in this picture, are seen from one level, the hills and sky from a different level.

The diagram shows how this picture would be limited, as seen from normal eye level by mechanical perspective projection.

RAY BETHERS: Sunday

RAOUL DUFY: Les Pêcheurs à la Ligne, *Courtesy Perls Galleries*

Counteracting the Faults of Perspective

IN THIS EARLY PAINTING, Raoul Dufy has successfully counteracted the strong perspective direction leading the eye out of the picture at the left side—not only by the counteracting positions of the boats and figures, but also by his use of opposing curved lines in the fishing poles.

Hogarth's *False Perspective* gives a very good idea of perspective, but in reverse. He has endeavored to show as many perspective errors as possible, as close examination will show. Oddly enough, many modern painters, to lessen the space effects in their pictures, will sometimes use a reversal of perspective, somewhat as Hogarth did, but not for the same reason.

[94]

HOGARTH: False Perspective

Oriental Space Conception

THE CHINESE PAINTERS have known about Italian mechanical perspective since as long ago as the Seventeenth Century, but have preferred their own methods for representing the idea of space.

This East Indian painting is similar to the Chinese in conception, showing space by *parallel* recession, rather than by perspective, with its converging lines. In this picture, space is achieved not only by parallel receding lines but by the overlapping of planes as well. Objects overlap from front to back, in a space movement leading from lower right to upper left. The drawing is isometric (without convergence) to a great extent, especially in the houses. The line relationships are composed of a simple combination of two diagonals, combined with horizontal and vertical directions. This arrangement is planned not only for space, but for pattern as well. While recession is shown, objects at the top, and consequently farther away, do not get smaller, but stay on the picture plane for that reason. This conception of space has also been used in much Occidental painting, both old and new.

EAST INDIAN, MUGHAL: The Spy Zunbur Brings Mahiyya into Town. *Courtesy of the Metropolitan Museum of Art*

Pattern Combined with Space

Most works of art combine flat pattern with the idea of space; the two-dimensional pattern integrated with the three-dimensional space. This is difficult to see, at times, but even so, it is much more important that the picture be experienced as a whole.

These simple diagrams show the fundamental principles of space-pattern combination:

Number 1 is pattern only, on a flat surface, without space. In Number 2, by the rearrangement of planes to overlap, space is shown, and some of the pattern is lost. But by the arrangement, in Number 3, space and geometric pattern have been combined. To the same arrangement, in Number 4, transparency has been added, which eliminates the space and brings everything back to the picture plane.

In Christopher Wood's painting, note how the curving lines of the cliff and wall not only recede in space, but are so designed as to act as pattern on the picture plane as well.

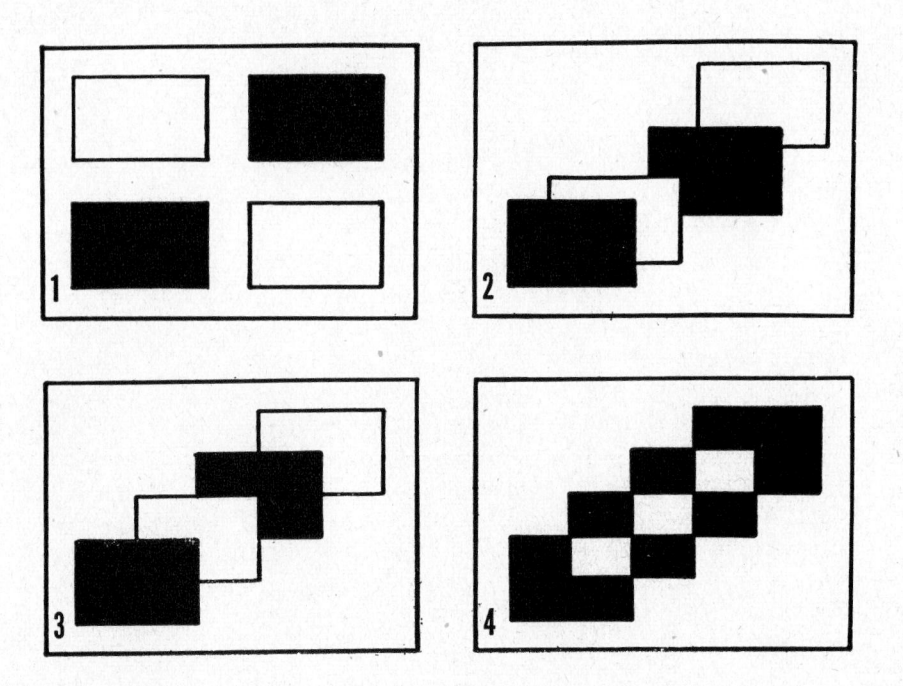

CHRISTOPHER WOOD: Tréboul (Church and Harbor). *Photograph courtesy of the American British Art Center, Inc., New York*

Equivocal Space

"EQUIVOCAL," according to the dictionary, means "susceptible of different interpretations." Thus it is with equivocal space, space which can be interpreted in two ways. This is an old idea in painting, found in the early Persians; Fra Angelico used it in the Fifteenth Century, as do many painters today.

Morris Davidson has written the following explanation of equivocal space, as used in his still-life painting on the opposing page:

"In this still life there are depicted, from the top down, a bowl and liquor bottle, a plaster cast of a hand, another bottle, a vase, and a fish. The dark *vertical* plane on the right side of the vase is also a *horizontal* plane on the table, hence equivocal. The black cast shadow of the hand is also the bottom of the liquor bottle. The patterns throughout are independent of the objects so that a tone will at one moment appear on the object and at the next assert a meaning of its own in the design.

"Note for example the triangular gray pattern linking the right corner of the bowl, label on the bottle, and plane of the hand. The constant shift in meaning through change of emphasis is the value of equivocal space-painting, since it is renewed relationships which hold the interest, not picturization of objects."

Morris Davidson: Still Life with Fish

Transparency and Interpenetration

THIS IS AN EFFECT peculiar to painting, although something similar may sometimes be found in nature. It is fantasy, in one way; a method of showing more than the eye can see. In another way, transparency and interpenetration can be used to reduce space, to bring a drawing into closer relation with its picture plane.

Chagall, in his *I and the Village*, uses these principles for fantasy as well as integration. Note how the plane, extending up from lower left, brings the distant figures forward to the picture plane.

In this early Cubist painting, by Jean Metzinger, transparency and interpenetration are used to flatten the picture, as well as to produce both a "deep" and "flat" treatment of the objects shown.

MARC CHAGALL: I and the Village. *Collection of the Museum of Modern Art, New York*

JEAN METZINGER: Still Life with Cigarettes. *Collection of Walter Pach; photograph courtesy Jacques Seligmann and Co. Inc.*

Art Is Not a Copy of Nature (II)

HERE IS A LANDSCAPE composition by Cézanne, and a photograph taken of the motif, where he painted the picture. It is impossible to say *why* Cézanne made these changes from the actual world, but certain pictorial effects are evident, and it is well known that Cézanne did not paint for descriptive reasons alone.

In the first place, he has raised the level of the hill, which fills the format in a more satisfactory manner, and gives more height than is shown in the photograph.

The receding road—a triangular directional shape which recedes strongly into the photograph as well as pushing outward—has been brought into two-dimensional relationship with the picture plane, the right side reaffirming the vertical, and the left the horizontal lines of the format. Also, the strong diagonal line from upper left, down through the road to lower right in the photograph, has been eliminated by rearrangement in design. In addition, a rhythmic movement has been woven throughout the picture, in contrast to the static effect of the photograph.

A more complete comparison of this motif and painting will be found in Erle Loran's excellent book, *Cézanne's Composition.*

Photograph of the Motif by John Rewald

PAUL CÉZANNE: La Route Tournante. *Collection of the Smith College Museum of Art, Northampton, Massachusetts*

[105]

Translating from the Actual World

THIS IS AN OUTLINE intended to show some differences between the "actual" world and a picture which translates this world of three dimensions into the idea of three dimensions on a flat plane.

These two ideas are somewhat foreign to each other. Movement, for instance, as it takes place in the world of actuality covers a period of time, but as seen in a picture is necessarily static.

The following is a general idea, rather than specific, of the difference between actuality and pictures, rather than between actuality and a work of art.

ACTUAL WORLD	PICTURES
Movement	*Movement*
The actual world is composed of movement through space, in any or all directions. Movement may be continuous, and part of this may be only remembered movement.	A picture is necessarily static, and while action can be indicated, it must be done with the aid of devices such as rhythm, directional lines, arrangement of planes, etc.
Field of Vision	*Field of Vision*
It is possible to be aware of space in all directions. However, in actual seeing, it is only possible to focus the eyes on one plane in space at one time. Remembered seeing is usually a *series* of visual impressions.	A picture is limited entirely to the format, with the idea of space artificially achieved. Rhythmic lines and directions are sometimes used to unify a picture, and prevent it from appearing only as a fragment of nature.
Space and Volume	*Space and Volume*
Actual volume is seen in space with our two eyes, a "seeing around." This gives a sense of "roundness" of volumes. The sense of space and distance relationships in nature is aided by this fact, as well as by the memory of former experience in having traveled a similar distance in space before.	Space in pictures is purely an idea, existing as it does on a flat plane. Space differences here are seen simultaneously, without need to change the focus of the eyes. Space is created by overlapping, perspective, etc., volume by the use of light and shade, or arbitrary shading in following form.

Light and Color Range

In the actual world, light and color are almost unlimited. The differences range between the lightest color in full sunlight, to the darkest color in complete darkness.

Light and Color Range

Pictures employ artificial color and value relations to approximate the light and color of actuality. For instance, a very light color placed against a very dark one is necessary to produce a contrast similar to that in nature.

This arbitrary scale approximates the range of light and color in the actual world, as compared to the limited possibilities of pigment used in pictures.

Light and Color Range, Actual World

Light and Color Range,
Pigment

I Compose a Picture

Some years ago, I made a pencil sketch of a small church in Sonoma, California, and later from this sketch, painted this picture, *Sunday*, shown on the opposite page. At the time, it went the rounds of exhibitions, and it is not until now that I recapitulate on how this picture was painted.

It is used here because it is neither completely factual nor completely abstract, but lies somewhere in between. A description of this picture in the usual literary terms might be something like this: "It is Sunday, a quiet restful day in the country. The villagers are walking slowly to their hour of worship, reminded of the past by the gravestones in the lonely churchyard."

Now, as I painted this picture, nothing was further from my thoughts than this. Neither was I interested in a pictorial description of the church itself, but purely in painting a picture as a picture. The title, *Sunday*, was added much later.

On the following four pages, the composing of this picture is described in words and diagrams. Not the various stages and experiments that are part of every picture, but rather as an outline of why the picture developed as it did.

This picture has also been used for diagramming purposes through the book, to explain many ideas connected with picture making. It is interesting to note that the literary description describes almost all of the different versions of this picture, as far as *what is taking place—the scene* —is concerned, but each version shown requires a new, specific description to describe it in a *pictorial* way.

Ray Bethers: Sunday

1. *The church itself*. This photograph stands for the accidental effects in nature, completely impersonal, and without pictorial relationships of any kind.

2. *The sketch*. Made in pencil, directly from the church, with only a slight element of design; it has been somewhat simplified but still contains a great many factual details.

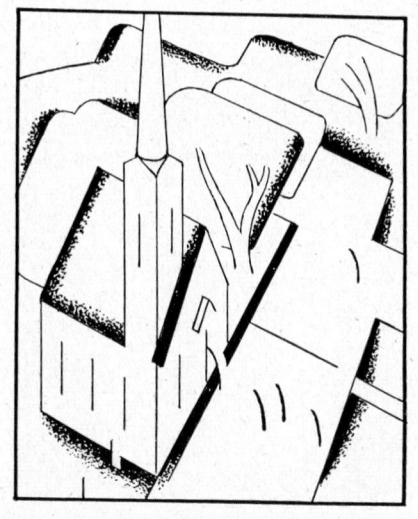

5. *Opposing diagonals* were developed to counterbalance the first two diagonals, which were parallel, related in space, but otherwise out of balance.

6. *Staccato pattern* of windows and figures superimposed on diagonal arrangement. New diagonal makes *two* areas of the road, too long and out of relationship otherwise.

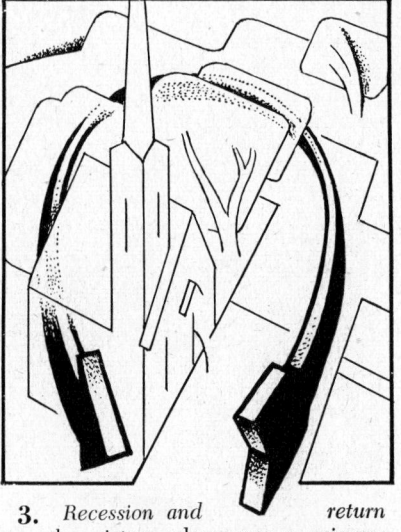

3. *Recession and* **   *return*** to the picture plane was a primary consideration; to provide an eye track, a path to explore the picture, and relate forms to one another.

4. *Tensions* and line relationships in space, as indicated by these two lines, are also related to one another as diagonals on the picture plane.

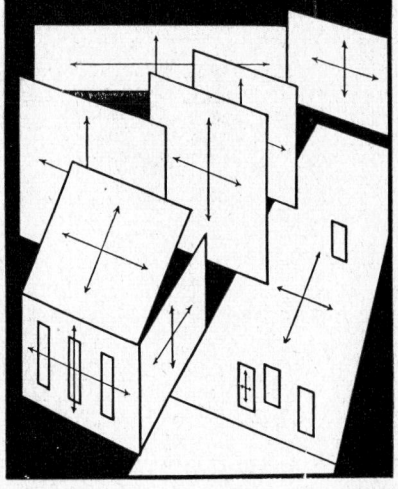

7. *Planes in space.* Planes are usually unseen in themselves, used to establish forms and directions in space, in relation to the picture plane.

8. *The final picture.* The looking-down view was arrived at to show recession into space more clearly, and to fill the format with forms rather than empty sky.

9. *Change in values* only, on the same drawing, gives a different pictorial effect. Note how the use of shadow creates new patterns in the total composition.

10. *Change in viewpoint.* Here the vantage point is from *below*, rather than above, a matter of selection only, but can still be described in the same literary terms as the original picture.

11. *Flat pattern,* as might be used for textiles or wallpaper, has only *two* dimensions; forms seen only from the front or from above, without recession in space.

12. *Transparency and interpenetration,* where a more complex pattern is combined with space. These diagrams show only a few of the countless ways of interpreting this same subject.

Paintings and Motif Photographs

THE COMPARISON between photographs and paintings, both made from the same position in relation to the subject, can often give great insight into a painter's thoughts and methods of working.

Eleven of these motif-painting comparisons follow; and beginning with Hiroshige, the pictures are arranged in approximate chronological order. In the case of Stuart Davis, two paintings are shown, one with its motif photograph, and a second painting which was developed some years later from the first one. In the Utrillo, while it is impossible to say, the comparison would indicate that the postcard was the actual motif.

Discounting the print by Hiroshige, and beginning with Corot, this series becomes still another version of "from realism to abstraction" over a period of time. Not that Hiroshige doesn't fit into this progression; he was just ahead of his time in this regard.

These comparisons are presented without further comment; the changes made from motif to painting tell much more than words can do.

Photograph of the Motif

HIROSHIGE

Photograph of the Motif by John Rewald

J. B. C. COROT: Island of San Bartolomeo. *Courtesy of the Museum of Fine Arts, Boston*

Photograph of the Motif from John Rewald

CLAUDE MONET: Rochers à Belle-Isle. Photograph courtesy of Durand-Ruel

Photograph of the Motif by John Rewald

CAMILLE PISSARRO: Les Toits du Vieux Rouen. *Private collection; photograph courtesy of Durand-Ruel*

Photograph of the Motif by John Rewald

Vincent van Gogh: Bridge of Trinquetaille. *Collection of Siegfried Kramarsky, New York*

Photograph of the Motif by Erle Loran; *from* Cézanne's Composition, *by Erle Loran. University of California Press*

PAUL CÉZANNE: Gardanne. Collection of Mr. and Mrs. F. H. Hirsch-land, New York

Photograph of the Motif from a Postcard

MAURICE UTRILLO: Chartres Cathedral. *Collection of Mr. and Mrs. Lloyd Bruce Wescott; photograph courtesy of the Museum of Modern Art, New York*

Photograph of the Motif

CHAIM SOUTINE: Chartres Cathedral. *Collection of Mr. and Mrs. Lloyd Bruce Wescott; photograph courtesy of the Museum of Modern Art, New York*

Another Photograph of the Motif, in the Summer

Photograph of the Motif (Rockport, Mass.). *Courtesy of
the Museum of Modern Art, New York*

STUART DAVIS: Summer Landscape, 1930. *Collection of the Museum of Modern Art, New York*

STUART DAVIS: Landscape in the Colors of a Pear, 1940. *Cranbrook Museum of Art*

Photograph of the Motif, *from A. Dorner,* THE WAY BEYOND "ART," *courtesy of Wittenborn, Schultz, Inc.*

HERBERT BAYER: Window by the Desk, *from A. Dorner,* THE WAY BEYOND "ART," *courtesy of Wittenborn, Schultz, Inc.*

Photograph of the Motif, *from* Picasso, the Recent Years, *by Harriet and Sidney Janis. Doubleday*

[136]

PABLO PICASSO: Le Vert-Galant, *from* PICASSO, THE RECENT YEARS, *by Harriet and Sidney Janis. Doubleday*

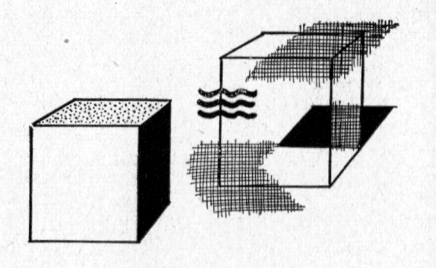

Two Broad Divisions of Pictures

ALMOST ANY PICTURE will correspond to certain principles in one of these two pictures. Not that one method is better than the other, but only that each is different in original conception.

1. In *St. Nicholas and the Three Youths*, the composition is formed by the shape of the objects themselves, in relation to one another. There is a certain amount of light and shade, but it is used primarily to describe the actual forms.

2. In Jon Corbino's *Eclipse*, the light and dark pattern is independent of the individual forms, the dark and light being utilized to unify the total picture rather than to describe forms individually.

Bicci di Lorenzo (1373-1452): St. Nicholas and the Three Youths. *Courtesy of the Metropolitan Museum of Art*

Jon Corbino: The Eclipse. *Photograph courtesy of the Kleemann Galleries*

[139]

Two Kinds of Proportion

GLENN WESSELS SAYS, "One may divide all painting into two kinds: in one the attempt is limited to the accurate copying of optical appearances, in the other the attempt is to *interpret* optical appearances and to express the artist's idea or concept of the subject matter in terms of the artistic medium. The total quantity of conceptual art in the world far outweighs the amount of appearance art, for only in periods of spiritual decadence, when materialism is rampant, has much that is merely optical drawing and painting appeared. In the great constructive periods of faith and confidence the painters have found (along with Spinoza) that 'only contemplated experience is real'—that pictorial reality is a thing of the understanding and spirit and not of the eye alone. The art of such periods is related to universal principles of structure rather than to superficial skill in the production of tricky illusions.

"The art of the Egyptians, the Greeks, the Byzantines and of the early and middle Italian Renaissance—although often different in many other respects—was conceptual art, and so was that of the great periods in the Orient. One outworking of the conceptual attitude which is found in all of them is a characteristic treatment of the relative proportion of far and near forms. Size was determined by true importance and not by accidental appearance.

"The eye alone says that a far-away mountain peak is a mole-hill and a near foothill is a mountain. The mind refuses this false evidence and recognizes the distant mountain as truly monumental and the near foothill as comparatively small. The great oriental artist and the contemporary painter are alike in their refusal to accept the dictates of an optical-mechanical perspective which produces psychological untruths. They paint what they see only when it is informed by what they know and feel. In the case of the far mountain and the near foothill, this produces an effect of just proportion and orderly size relationship which makes possible the compositional rhythm necessary to a successful picture."

Tsao Jun: Chinese Landscape Painting. *Courtesy of the Metropolitan Museum of Art*

Boardman Robinson: Mountain Anatomy. *Photograph courtesy of the Kraushaar Galleries*

[141]

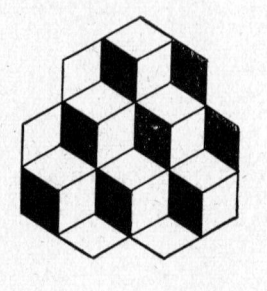

Illusion

ILLUSION IN PAINTING is only an optical trick, to produce a puzzle picture, and has absolutely no relation to painting as a fine art. It is not new, and neither is it good nor bad in a picture.

Anyone who draws can do it, simply by a double use of values. Seen in one way, the value forms an image, while, at the same time, the same value and shape represent an object or part of an object differing in subject from that formerly seen.

For example: the target, in the lower picture, seen in one way, is only a target. But in combination with other subject-form-value relationships, it becomes a human eye. Illusionistic or double-image pictures must be evaluated on the broader principles of all fine arts, rather than by judging only on illusionistic subject matter.

SALVADOR DALI: Old Age, Adolescence, and Infancy

TRADITION OF ARCIMBOLDO (16th Century): Landscape-Head.
*Private collection, photograph courtesy of the Museum of Modern
Art, New York*

[143]

Line Direction: The Vertical Line as a Dominant

A LINE, A SHAPE, or a direction is capable of making us feel an emotion. A very tall building, a tree, a Gothic cathedral, all have in common the quality of verticality, but none can be said to have a "subject." They just are.

As Charles Lindstrom * points out, there is a connection between "vertical and virtue." Church steeples have been reaching skyward for centuries. An "upright" man is another example.

Both pictures opposite, quite isolated from each other in time, are unified by the repeated use of the vertical, reaffirming the larger vertical of their format. Note also that both pictures are quite Gothic in feeling.

* *What Makes Art Work?* by Charles Lindstrom. Booklet, now out of print. San Francisco Museum of Art. 1940.

BONFIGLI (1454-1496): Funeral of Sant'
Ercolano. *Pinacoteca Vanucci, Perugia*

PAUL KLEE: Strange Hunt. 1937.
*Photograph courtesy of the Nieren-
dorf Gallery*

The Horizontal Line

THE ACTUAL HORIZON, seen far away, is always peaceful and gives forth a quiet and restful feeling. A fallen object is horizontal; it has come to rest. At the seashore, it is a common desire to imitate the horizon, to relax, to lie at ease on the sand.

In pictures, a dominant horizontal feeling may bring forth a similar emotion, regardless of the picture's subject, as can be realized from Neroccio de' Landi's *The Battle of Actium*.

The horizontal and vertical directions are extremely important in composition, as both repeat and reaffirm the fundamental lines of the format.

Though neither this diagram nor these pictures illustrate the fact, the horizontal is not necessarily a quiet line but can be a "speed" line instead.

[146]

NEROCCIO·DE' LANDI (1447-1500): The Battle of Actium. *National Gallery of Art, Washington, D.C., Kress Collection*

DONG KINGMAN: Two Boats on a River, 1942. *Collection of Mr. and Mrs. Ralph R. Knoblaugh, photograph courtesy of the Midtown Galleries, New York*

The Diagonal Line

THE DIAGONAL IS off balance. Not many pic-
tures are based on the diagonal alone, for that very reason. A strong
diagonal is usually opposed by a similar diagonal, acting as a brace to
restore balance to the picture. The diagonal is also a *space* line, and if
not falling, may then lie on the surface of a receding plane. It is very
often used for a dual purpose, in combining space with pattern.

In considering all of these dominants, and there are many more than
are shown here, a strong direction can also be indicated by a series of
shorter related lines combined in one dominant direction or rhythm.
Also, a line or direction will sometimes "jump" across an area, to be
picked up by another direction. This effect is usually called a *subjective
line*.

WILLIAM BLAKE (1757-1827): The Wise and Foolish Virgins. *Courtesy of the Metropolitan Museum of Art*

JOSÉ CLEMENTE OROZCO: Zapatistas, 1931. *Collection of the Museum of Modern Art, New York*

[149]

The Triangle

THE TRIANGLE evolves from architecture, as many pictorial forms do, as a fundamental principle of construction. A triangle is stable, equally braced on all three sides.

Although these two pictures are widely separated, both in style and time, they are basically the same in the unifying use of the triangle.

SANDRO BOTTICELLI (1444-1510): Last Communion. *Courtesy of the Metropolitan Museum of Art*

CANDIDO PORTINARI: Scarecrow, 1940. *Collection of the Museum of Modern Art, New York*

Opposing Diagonals

Opposing lines will "cross themselves out"; they counterbalance one another. In one way, they are in conflict; yet, collectively, they balance, and lie on the picture plane.

No matter what line or lines are dominant in a picture, secondary directions will always be found. But pictures, in their smaller areas, are usually designed in a similar way to the larger forms. It is this principle that unifies the total picture, causing "first things to be seen first," secondary areas later. It is also one quality that differentiates a work of art from a photograph or from a purely factual picture.

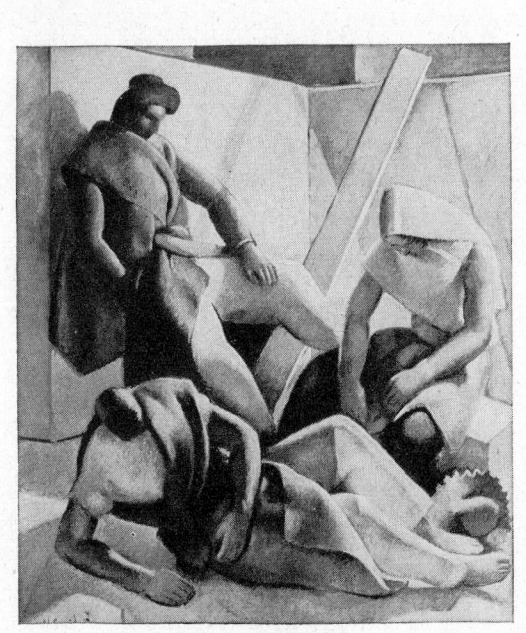

GHEERAERT DAVID (1450?-1523): Deposition. *Copyright the Frick Collection, New York*

ALFREDO GUIDO: Stevedores Resting, 1938. *Collection of the Museum of Modern Art, New York*

[153]

The Balanced Square

This could also be called opposing diagonals, but the actual designation is not important. But it is important to recognize the similarity of geometric foundation in these two compositions.

EL GRECO (1541-1614): Christ Bearing the Cross. *Madrid, Prado*

JUAN GRIS: Still Life, 1911. *Collection of the Museum of Modern Art, New York*

[155]

The Curving Line

A CURVE IS RHYTHMIC, a moving, dancing line. A picture based on a curving line is apt to contain many other related curves, with angular forms subordinated. Gaiety, movement, and action are often expressed in related curving lines.

EL GRECO (1541-1614): Expulsion from the Temple. *Copyright the Frick Collection*

FLETCHER MARTIN: Trouble in 'Frisco, 1938. *Collection of the Museum of Modern Art, New York*

Horizontal, Vertical, and Diagonal Lines

ALL PICTURES are a combination of many directional lines, some dominant and others subordinated.

In Pieter Breughel's *The Huntsmen in the Snow*, the quiet horizontal line is opposed to a vertical pattern and, as can be seen, the diagonal movement from lower left to upper right creates a spatial feeling.

Johannes Schiefer's *Mamaroneck Harbor* has been composed on a very similar plan, although quite different in subject and in surface treatment. For better comparison, this picture has been reversed, as though seen in a mirror. This reversal does not affect the composition in any way. Most painters study their unfinished pictures in this manner, which can be recommended for the fresh viewpoint it gives to any picture.

PIETER BREUGHEL (1525-1569): The Huntsmen in the Snow. *Vienna Museum*

JOHANNES SCHIEFER: Mamaroneck Harbor, 1946. *Photograph courtesy of the Kleemann Galleries, New York*

Distortion for Integration

A FRIEND ONCE SAID, "I can understand exaggeration, but not distortion," which is, after all, only a question of degree and definition. Distortion has come to mean a slightly unpleasant quality in drawing, and the word "conditioning" has sometimes been used in its place.

In many pictures, natural forms have been "conditioned," elongated for instance, the same effect of elongation being used throughout the picture. This gives all elements a certain pictorial and rhythmic unity, a collective vertical direction similar to the use of the vertical line. It is compositional principles like these that photography cannot imitate, when each form is conditioned in relation to every other element in the picture.

El Greco has sometimes in the past been wrongly suspected of astigmatism, or other eye affliction, by people who lack an understanding of his use of pictorial distortion.

EL GRECO (1541-1614): *Detail from
The Two Saints John. Toledo, Iglesia
de los Padres Jesuitas*

AMEDEO MODIGLIANI: Portrait d'une
Jeune Femme. *Courtesy of the Perls
Galleries, New York*

Caricature

CARICATURE IS THE ART of emphasis, of more real than real, and is usually achieved by a certain degree of abstraction. The intensity of caricature is not brought about by overemphasis of features already evident, as is done in some so-called "cartoons," but rather by a series of synthesized and unified relationships, in the drawing as a whole.

Caricature is not an isolated quality by any means, but is one of the basic principles of painting as a fine art, a conditioning of form to the end desired.

The power in Kaethe Kollwitz's lithograph comes largely from what might be called caricature, the violent action arising from the sweep of writhing lines from above, is violent by relationship to the curving lines of the children below.

Sotomayor's use of lines related to an elongated oval has almost a centrifugal force. Note the extreme simplification, especially the relationship of the one eye and nose to the entire head.

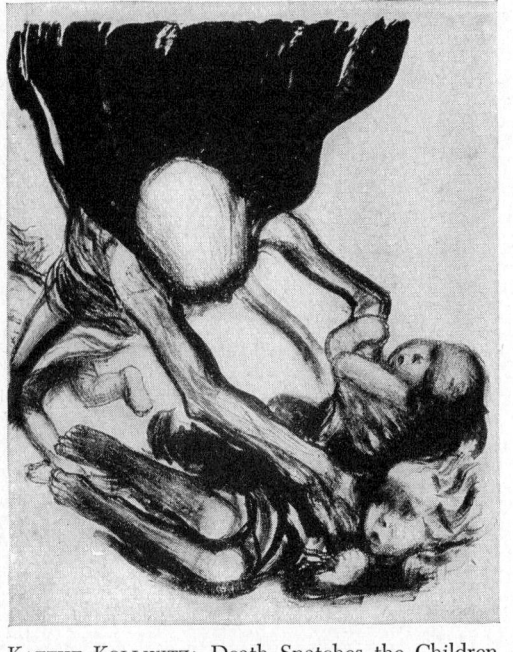

KAETHE KOLLWITZ: Death Snatches the Children.
Collection of the Museum of Modern Art, New York

SOTOMAYOR: Caricature

[163]

Abstraction

Edward wadsworth, the British painter, once said, "A picture is primarily the animation of an inert plane surface by a spatial rhythm of forms and colors."

That describes this diagram of a "pure abstraction," as it does many other kinds of pictures. As emotionally and intellectually conceived by an artist, a "pure abstraction" is a painting without *another* subject; it *is* the subject.

In this case, there is a general rotary movement which begins at the lower left, and continues on around the format. Note how the larger forms are related in proportion to the negative shapes of the dark background.

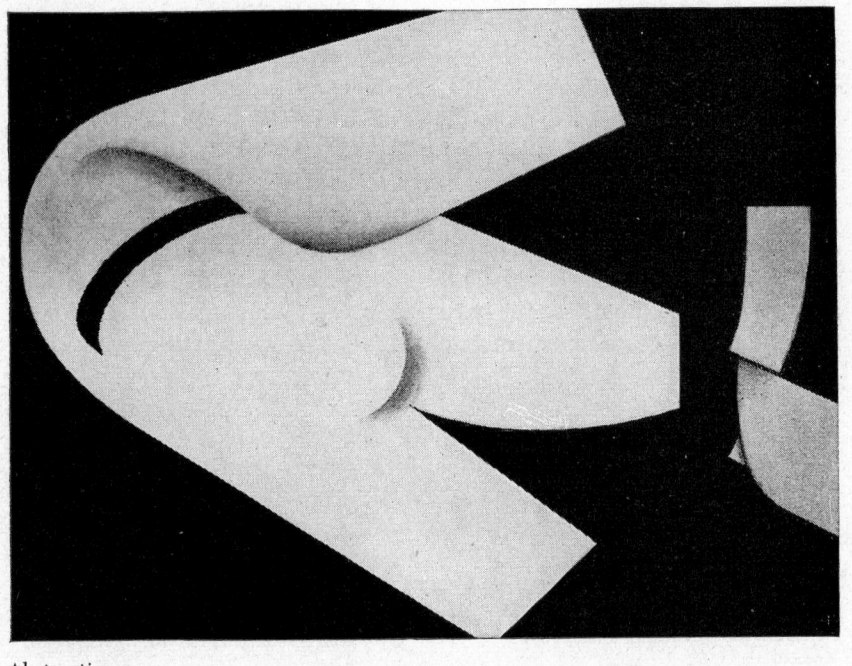

Abstraction

Abstraction for Unification

W HILE THE "pure abstraction" on the preced-
ing page was only a diagram, it is, in effect, the structure of this Fifteenth-
Century *Portrait of a Lady*. Abstraction, in this sense, is certainly not
new; all artists from the beginning of time have unified pictures by other
means than those of subject alone. The abstraction unifying this picture
is that which is left when the subject has been eliminated.

Abstraction in painting is usually arrived at in the following ways:

1. Evolved out of the subject during actual painting.

2. Conceived first, and combined with the subject.

3. As an end in itself, the painting being "non-objective," or "pure
abstraction," and having no forms or subject taken from the actual world.

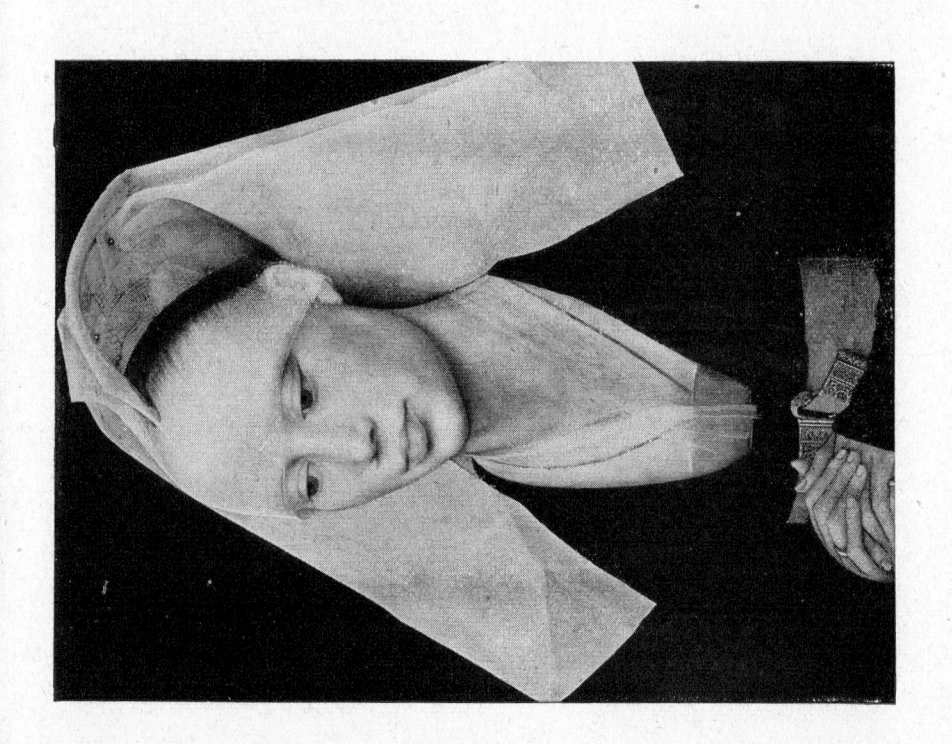

Rogier van der Weyden (1400-1464): Portrait of a Lady. *National Gallery of Art, Washington, D.C., Mellon Collection*

Looking for Abstraction

MOST PAINTERS, during the process of composing a picture, will often look at their uncompleted picture upside down. This gives a fresh viewpoint and, what is most important, allows the picture to be seen without the influence of its subject.

Why not try this yourself, when possible, and turn a picture upside down to understand the formal construction more clearly, to see the abstract elements used for pictorial unification?

RUSSELL COWLES: Rainy Day. *Photograph courtesy of the Kraushaar Galleries*

[169]

Abstraction Derived from the Subject

THIS PICTURE is both realistic and abstract. The ships are drawn in a factual manner, but are unified by the over-all abstract camouflage pattern. Camouflage, itself, is a form of abstraction; its purpose being to destroy form by resolving one form into another, thereby confusing the total form. It is really a reversal of "first things first," in the principle of unification, as applied to a work of art.

In this picture, the camouflage shapes have been utilized as pattern, to relate the two ships to each other and to the picture as a whole.

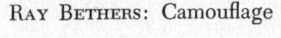

RAY BETHERS: Camouflage

Abstraction as an End in Itself

Since terminology in art is so confused, "pure abstraction" must also be remembered as being "non-objective"—a picture without a subject, and unrelated to objects in the actual world.

Mondrian has, perhaps, carried "pure abstraction" as far as any painter —to an arrangement of horizontal and vertical lines on a plane surface, a two-dimensional picture without space.

It is difficult to comment on this picture; but my own point of view is this: when painting becomes as abstract and geometric as it has with Mondrian, it begins to approach architecture in space division, and is, perhaps, no longer pictorial. But it is a definite contribution, and much can be learned from Mondrian's experiments.

PIET MONDRIAN: Composition in Black, White, and Red. Collection of the Museum of Modern Art, New York

Diagrammed Paintings

Iɴ ᴅɪᴀɢʀᴀᴍᴍɪɴɢ ᴛʜᴇsᴇ ᴘɪᴄᴛᴜʀᴇs, the aim has been to get beneath the surface, beyond the subject, to the abstract geometric quality that organizes each picture.

Accent in the diagrams has been placed on the dark forms, as was done by the artists themselves in their pictures. Nothing has been added, but forms have been simplified and their directions clarified, in the hope that the construction of these and other pictures will be more easily realized.

Sandro Botticelli

To UNIFY the long format in *Three Miracles of St. Zenobius,* Botticelli has used fluid, dancing lines in the foreground—lines that move across and unite the three groups into one. Opposed to these are the regularly spaced verticals, the pattern of windows and the diagonals as used to describe both space and pattern.

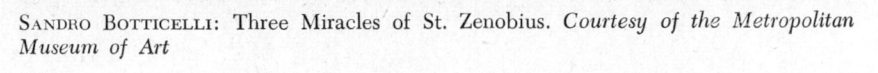

SANDRO BOTTICELLI: Three Miracles of St. Zenobius. *Courtesy of the Metropolitan Museum of Art*

[177]

Pieter Breughel

HERE IS A remarkably organized picture. A strong diagonal moves through space, from lower left to upper right, where it is turned back into the picture again by the angular mountain forms. Opposing this is the upper-left to lower-right diagonal, turned again at the lower right, and up into the picture. As a minor note, observe the placing of the four birds and the curved branches leading down into space.

PIETER BREUGHEL: The Huntsmen in the Snow. *Vienna Museum*

El Greco

I<small>N</small> *Christ Bearing the Cross*, El Greco has utilized a balanced square, a series of opposing diagonals. The projecting cross has been foreshortened and incorporated into the dominant diagonal arrangement; otherwise it would come forward of the picture plane. Even the halo, usually shown as circular, has been conditioned to the general plan.

EL GRECO: Christ Bearing the Cross.
Madrid, Prado

Georges Seurat

THIS GREAT PAINTING is dominantly horizontal with secondary vertical directions. The shadow in the foreground has a rectangular-shaped light spot which locates this entire plane in space.

Notice the methods used by Seurat in moving the eye around the four corners.

In the upper center of the picture is a woman with an umbrella, walking beside a child. The skirt and child are almost lost in a value similar to their background, hence only the upper part of the woman's body registers as part of the picture's organization.

GEORGES SEURAT: Afternoon on Grande Jatte Island. *Courtesy of the Art Institute of Chicago, Helen Birch Bartlett Memorial Collection*

[183]

Emil Ganso

THIS IS AN EXAMPLE of an elliptical eye track in pictorial space. Your eye will probably enter at the lower left, follow up the angular river, then left up the hill, to return down the road again; or it is easily possible to go the other way round. In either case, there is a great deal of optical exploration possible in this picture due to its particular arrangement of directional lines.

EMIL GANSO: Winter Morning. *From the Permanent Gallery of the State University of Iowa, photograph courtesy of the Weyhe Gallery*

[185]

Native Arts

THE CREATION of a work of art is not limited to the graduates of art schools. Art existed long before art training was ever thought of.

While a great many so-called principles of painting are named and isolated from each other in this book, it does not necessarily follow that the creator of a work of art is conscious of these "principles," or is able to call them by name. That comes later when the picture is finished and it is then found that some elements have been used before, by others, to gain the same effect. After all, every composer in music begins with the same notes as raw material; it is in his personal way of arranging these notes that a work of art is born.

Native painters, isolated geographically as they are, produce works of art which, fundamentally, are in no way different from other great works, and can be observed in the same manner.

In fact, these artists will usually work from a fresh and uncluttered point of view, an advantage not common in our modern world. However, there are also traditions in tribal arts, as well as in our own. Many modern painters have used the same space and pattern conception as this Balinese artist, who has combined space, pattern, and texture to an amazing degree.

GUSTI KAMPIANG: Kampoeng. *Native Balinese Painting in the author's collection*

Children's Painting

Monica HALEY, Art Supervisor for the Richmond (California) Child Care Center, has made some interesting observations from her varied experience in teaching children to paint. She says:

"Regardless of socio-economic backgrounds or racial differences, each child, if allowed spontaneous free expression, expresses himself in easel painting in distinct stages. At the age of two his expressions are apparent in a scribble in which vertical lines and splash-dots predominate. Later the horizontals develop. At the age of three years and six months the child adds to these expressions concise circles clockwise and counter clockwise. The late threes put together irregular areas of color covering the page. The four-year-olds, regardless of previous experience, assemble verticals and horizontals into neat abstract arrangements, with carefully directed splash-dots forming part of the design. During the early part of the fourth year a chief characteristic of design is a continuous line of contrasting color segments moving in varied directions over the page.

"The artistic behavior patterns up to four and a half years constitute symbolic abstractions. Then attempted realism begins to develop through the early figure and house stage. The crude beginnings of figure representation continue to be augmented and added to so that by the end of the fifth year the child has ceased to express himself abstractly.

"The complicated theme stage marks the child's growth from self to greater awareness of environment. Trees, boats, animals, elaborate houses, airplanes, autos, playgrounds, groups of people, typify his expanding world. The development of this stage is apparent at the age of six and continues in elaboration and complication until the end of the child art period at the age of eleven or twelve."

DICK DENMAN (AGE 7): *Richmond Child Care Center*

VIKRAM (AGE 7): Explosion. *Bombay, India; Instructor, Emmy Lichtwitz-Krasso*

[189]

Folk Art

FOLK PAINTING is sometimes called "primitive painting," which in one way it is, but the term can easily be confused, since it is also applied to the painting of primitive tribes.

Folk paintings may or may not be contemporary, but are all painted by people with a fresh viewpoint, people who "just paint," who have something to say, and say it sometimes in a naïve manner, without previous professional training.

Having "something to say" is important in any phase of art, the technical method of saying being relatively unimportant. Perhaps folk painting is not among the greatest of art manifestations, but it is not to be passed over solely on account of the painter's technical deficiencies. Craftmanship is not necessarily one of the attributes of the art of painting.

CAMILLE BOMBOIS: La Chute d'Eau. *Courtesy of the Perls Galleries, New York*

NINA DAVIS: The Blacksmith's Shop. *Courtesy of the Harry Stone Gallery, New York*

Why Don't You Paint?

THERE IS NO BETTER WAY to understand painting than to do it yourself. With or without instruction, the actual painting of pictures will help in the understanding of all pictures, aside from the personal satisfaction to be found in creative work.

The actual process of painting is not difficult. With red, yellow, blue, black and white, a few brushes, and something to paint on, it is possible to create a work of art. Even a pencil and paper can be used creatively without technical training. The main thing is to paint, to express yourself and not be concerned with what people say about your efforts. A great many painters have been much criticized, but have gone on painting just the same.

Paul Gauguin was a "Sunday painter" until he was thirty-five. But in 1883, after ten years of married life, and despite the responsibility of five children, he gave up a successful banking career to become a full-time painter. However, one can paint without making such a drastic change.

PAUL GAUGUIN: The Moon and the Earth (Hina Tefatu). *Collection of the Museum of Modern Art, New York*

Painters on Art

MANY PAINTERS have written on their own paintings, and their personal views on the art of painting in general. The following section is composed of nine statements of this kind.

Paul Gauguin

"THE PAREO being an essential part of the life of the Tahitians, I use it for a bedspread. The stuff . . . has to be yellow, because that color suggests to the spectator the unexpected, and suggests a lit-lamp effect, which saves me the trouble of producing a lamplight effect. I need a rather awesome background. So violet is naturally indicated. And there is the musical part of my picture put together! . . . I see naught but terror. Now what kind? Assuredly not the terror of a Suzannah surprised by elders, for that kind does not exist in Oceania.

"The Tupapau (Spirit of the Dead) at once suggests itself. It is the constant dread of the Tahitians. At night, they keep a lamp burning. . . .

"Once I have hit on my Tupapau I stick to it and make it the motive of my picture, the nude being relegated to the background.

"What can be a Tahitian's notion of a ghost? She knows nothing of the stage, of novels, so, when she thinks of the dead she naturally thinks of some one she has already seen. Therefore, my ghost, my spirit must be some sort of an old woman.

"My decorative sense leads to my strewing flowers on the background. The Tupapau's flowers, phosphorescences, . . . are a sign that the spirit has you in mind. A Tahitian belief. . . .

"I recapitulate. The musical part: undulating horizontal lines; harmonies of orange and blue woven together by yellows and violets, their own derivative colors, and lightened by greenish sparkles. The literary part: the Spirit of a Living Girl united to the Spirit of the Dead. Night and Day.

"This explanation of the genesis of my picture is written for the benefit of those who always insist on knowing the why and wherefore of everything.

"In other respects, it is simply no more than a study of the nude in Oceania." *

* *Gauguin*, by Robert Rey. John Lane, The Bodley Head, London.

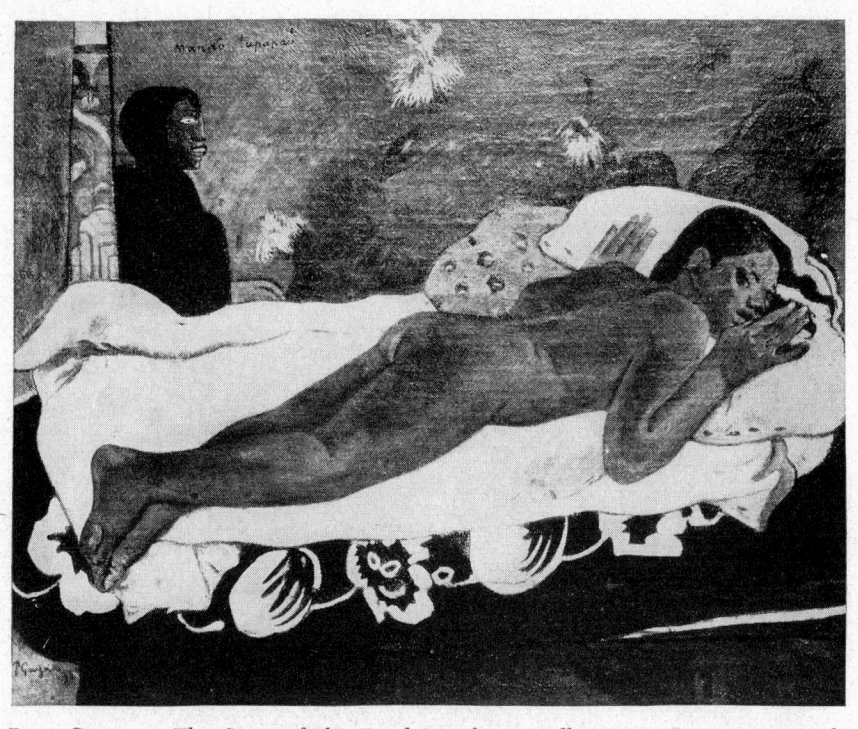

PAUL GAUGUIN: The Spirit of the Dead Watching. *Collection of A. Conger Good-year, New York; photograph courtesy of the Museum of Modern Art, New York*

Juan Gris

"I CONSIDER THAT THE architectural aspect of painting is mathematics, the abstract aspect. This I wish to humanize. Of a bottle, Cézanne made a cylinder. Of a cylinder, I make a bottle—a certain bottle. Cézanne's destination is architecture. Architecture is my point of departure. That is why I compose with abstractions (colors) and when these colors become objects I make adjustments. For instance, I compose with a black and with a white and I make adjustments when the white has become a piece of paper and the black a shadow. I mean to say that I adjust the white so that it becomes a piece of paper and the black so that it becomes a shadow." *

* Reprinted by permission of Peggy Guggenheim. *Art of This Century.* New York.

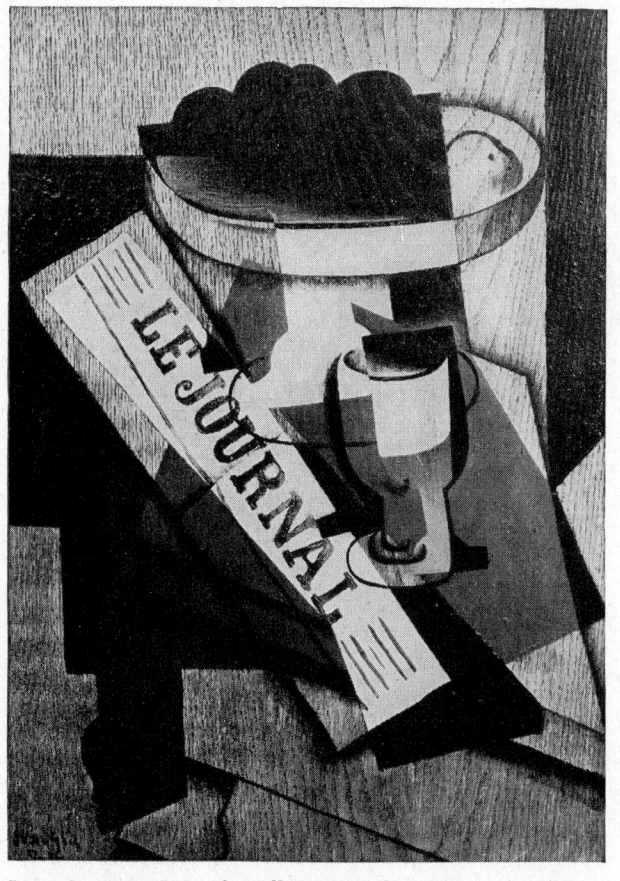

JUAN GRIS: Le Journal. *Collection of the Museum of Modern Art, New York*

Georges Braque

"IN ART PROGRESS consists not in the extension but in the knowledge of one's limitations.

"The limitation of the means employed gives the style, produces the new form and stimulates creation.

"The limitation of the means is often the reason for the charm and power of primary painting. On the other hand, the extension of the means brings about the various forms of decadent art.

"New means, new subjects.

"The subject is not the object but a new unity, the lyricism that projects beyond the means employed.

"A painter thinks in form and color.

"The aim of painting is not to reconstruct an anecdotal fact but to construct a pictorial fact.

"Painting is a method of representation.

"Do not imitate what you wish to create.

"The aspect cannot be imitated; the aspect is the result.

"To be a pure imitation painting must disregard the aspect.

"To paint from nature is to improvise. . . .

"Emotion should not be interpreted by emotional trembling. Emotion cannot be added to a painting nor can it be imitated. Emotion is the germ and the work of art is the birth.

"I believe in the law that serves to correct the emotions." *

* *Nord-Sud, Revue Littéraire* No. 10: December, 1917. Reprinted by permission of Peggy Guggenheim. *Art of This Century.* New York.

GEORGES BRAQUE: The Table. *Collection of the Museum of Modern Art, New York*

Henri Matisse

"I began at the École des Beaux Arts. When I opened my studio, years after, for some time I painted just like any one else. But things didn't go at all, and I was very unhappy. Then, little by little, I began to paint as I felt. One cannot do successful work which has much feeling unless one sees the subject very simply, and one must do this in order to express one's self as clearly as possible. . . .

"I certainly do think of harmony and color, and of composition, too. Drawing is for me the art of being able to express myself with line. When an artist or student draws a nude figure with painstaking care, the result is drawing, and not emotion. A true artist cannot see color which is not harmonious. Otherwise it is a *moyen,* or recipe. An artist should express his feeling with the harmony or idea of color which he possesses naturally. He should not copy the walls, or objects on a table, but he should, above all, express a vision of color, the harmony of which corresponds to his feeling. And, above all, one must be honest with one's self.

"If one *feels no emotion,* one should not paint." *

* Reprinted by permission from *Cubists and Post-Impressionism,* by Arthur Jerome Eddy. Chicago. A. C. McClurg & Co.

HENRI MATISSE: The Gourds. *Collection of the Museum of Modern Art, New York*

Wassily Kandinsky

"IN AN OBSCURE and puzzling way, the artist develops a work of art. As it gains a life of its own, it becomes an entity, an independent spiritual life, which as a being, leads the life of material realism. It is, therefore, not simply a phenomenon created casually and inconsequentially indifferent to spiritual life. Instead as a living being, it possesses creative active forces. It lives, has power, and actively forms the above-mentioned spiritual atmosphere. From an innermost point of view, the question finally should be answered as to whether creation is strong or weak. If too weak in its form, it is impotent to cause any kind of spiritual vibration.

"In reality, no picture can be considered 'well painted' if it possesses only correct tone values (the unavoidable *valeurs* of the French). One should call a picture well painted if it possesses the fullness of life. A 'perfect drawing' is the one where nothing can be changed without destroying the essential inner life, quite irrespective of whether this drawing contradicts our conception of anatomy, botany, or other sciences. The question is not whether the coincidental outer form is violated, but only, if its quality depends on the artist's need of certain forms irrespective of reality's pattern. Likewise, colours should be used not because they are true to nature but only because the colour harmony is required by the paintings individually. The artist is not only justified in using any form necessary for his purposes, but it is his very duty to do so. Neither anatomical correctness nor any basic overthrow of scientific statements are necessary, only the artist's unlimited freedom in the selection of his means." *

* From Wassily Kandinsky, *On the Spiritual in Art*. Published by the Solomon R. Guggenheim Foundation, for the Museum of Non-Objective Painting, New York City, 1946, Hilla Rebay, editor. Reprinted by permission.

WASSILY KANDINSKY: Composition VII, Fragment 1. *Collection of the Museum of Modern Art, New York*

Pablo Picasso

"A PICTURE IS NOT thought out and settled beforehand. While it is being done it changes as one's thoughts change. And when it is finished, it still goes on changing, according to the state of mind of whoever is looking at it. A picture lives a life like a living creature, undergoing the changes imposed on us by our life from day to day. This is natural enough, as the picture lives only through the man who is looking at it.

"At the actual time that I am painting a picture I may think of white and put down white. But I can't go on working all the time thinking of white and painting it. Colors, like features, follow the changes of the emotions. You've seen the sketch I did for a picture with all the colors indicated on it. What is left of them? Certainly the white I thought of and the green I thought of are there in the picture, but not in the places I intended, nor in the same quantities. Of course, you can paint pictures by matching up different parts of them so that they go quite nicely together, but they'll lack any kind of drama.

"I want to get to the stage where nobody can tell how a picture of mine is done. What's the point of that? Simply that I want nothing but emotion to be given off by it." *

* *Picasso: Forty Years of his Art,* edited by Alfred H. Barr, Jr. New York. Museum of Modern Art.

PABLO PICASSO: Woman in White.
*Collection of the Museum of
Modern Art, New York*

PABLO PICASSO: Seated Woman.
*Collection of the Museum of Mod-
ern Art, New York*

Joan Miro

"THE PLAY OF LINES and colors, if it does not lay bare the drama of the creator, is nothing more than a bourgeois pastime. The forms expressed by an individual attached to society should disclose the activity of a mind wishing to escape from present reality, which today is particularly ignoble, and seek out new realities, offering other men a possibility of elevation.

"If we do not attempt to discover the religious essence and magic meaning of things, we will do nothing but add new sources of brutishness to those which are offered today to countless peoples." *

* *Cahiers d'art, 1939.* Reprinted by permission of Peggy Guggenheim. *Art of This Century.* New York.

Joan Miró: Composition. Collection of the Museum of Modern Art, New York

Henry Moore: Sculptor

"For me a work must first have a vitality of its own. I do not mean a reflection of the vitality of life, of movement, physical action, frisking, dancing figures and so on, but that a work can have in it a pent-up energy, an intense life of its own, independent of the object it may represent. When a work has this powerful vitality we do not connect the word Beauty with it.

"Beauty in the later Greek or Renaissance sense, is not the aim of my sculpture.

"Between beauty of expression and power of expression there is a difference of function. The first aims at pleasing the senses, the second has a spiritual vitality which for me is more moving and goes deeper than the senses." *

* Henry Moore: Sculpture and Drawings, with an introduction by Herbert Read. Curt Valentin, New York; Percy Lund, Humphries & Co., Ltd., London, 1944.

HENRY MOORE: Group of Red Draped Figures. *Collection of Lois Orswell, photograph courtesy of the Buchholz Gallery*

Piet Mondrian

"NOT EVERYONE REALIZES that in all plastic art, even in the most naturalistic work, the natural form and color are always, to some extent, transformed. Actually while this may not be directly perceived, the tension of line and form, as well as the intensity of color are always increased. Plastic experience demonstrates that the natural appearance of things is not to be established in its essential realism, but must be transformed in order to evoke aesthetic sensation.

"In the course of centuries, the culture of plastic art has taught us that this transformation is actually the beginning of the abstraction of natural vision, which in modern times manifests itself as Abstract art. Although Abstract art has developed through the abstraction of the natural aspect, nevertheless in its present evolution it is more concrete because it makes use of pure form and pure color.

"Consciousness of the necessity of abstraction in plastic art was developed slowly. Originally it was practiced intuitively. Only after centuries of increasing transformation of the natural aspect, more apparent abstraction emerged, until finally plastic art was freed from the particular characteristics of subject and object. This liberation is of the greatest importance. For plastic art reveals that particular characteristics veil the pure expression of form, color and relationships. In plastic art, form and color are the essential expressive means. Their properties and mutual relationships determine the general expression of a work. Abstraction not only establishes form and color more objectively but also reveals their properties more clearly." *

* Reprinted by permission of Peggy Guggenheim. *Art of This Century.* New York.

PIET MONDRIAN: Composition in Gray, Blue, Yellow, and Red. *From a private collection; photograph courtesy of the Museum of Modern Art, New York.*

The Painters Write

THIS SECTION DIFFERS from the preceding one in that each artist has written, especially for this book, specific words about a specific picture, including some general viewpoints on the art of painting.

These viewpoints will be found to differ not only with each other, but some with this book as well. This is as it should be, as *all* artists are different from all others in how they feel, think, and paint. The painters who have written, have not seen this book; neither do they necessarily agree with the author's opinions.

In reading the words that follow, it should be remembered that the painter's *emotion* has already been expressed in *paint,* the words being explanatory rather than emotional, to the end that you may better understand their pictures.

Ansel Adams: Photographer

"BEFORE EXPOSURE of the negative I must visualize the final print. My creative concept is based on my response to the subject before me in space, and on the aggregate of emotional and intellectual experience back of me in time.

"I am seldom conscious of design, pattern, form, or any of the other 'constants' dear to critical hearts, until the picture has been completed. While critical analysis of completed works strengthens the ability to be aware and to perceive, the domination of restrictive compositional rules, modes, and manners *at the time of creation* may result in sterility of mood and creative insight.

"We must remember that the making of a photograph is an expressive adventure—usually a flash analytic perception of complex qualities. The painter is perhaps fortunate in that he may contemplate and synthesize over a considerable period of time; he may adjust, modulate and clarify as his work progresses. There is little the photographer can do—or should do, if he respects the integrity of his medium—after the exposure of the negative, for at that moment the final picture must be resolutely clear in his mind's eye. In the process of printing the negative he may perfect and clarify these dominant qualities; but the basic aspects of his photograph are predetermined and unalterable.

"The procedure of perception and execution is controlled by the personal instinctive connotations of various creative elements, some of which are: the 'rightness' of the viewpoint, wherefrom elements of the scene are clearly revealed in themselves and in relation to each other; the illusion of substance and the illusion of light, both qualities considered emotionally rather than factually; the impressions of scale and depth; the aspects which imply life and force and spiritual reality. Let all of these be distilled by emotional experience and the greatest reality evolves —that 'departure from reality' which, for the lack of a better term, is sometimes called art."

ANSEL ADAMS: Doors and Shutters (*photograph*)

Robert Benney

"THIS PAINTING, *Just Off the Line*, I began without reference to the sketch I had previously made during the battle of Saipan, for the memory of this wounded soldier was still very clear to me. It was not until after the painting was well laid in that I referred to my original drawing. I then found that my concept had since changed, and the sketch was of little value, except to recall the intensity of the moment.

"The idea I wanted to pictorially express was extreme loneliness, the loneliness of a severely wounded man far from home, to symbolize what war meant to the individual front-line soldier.

"My problem was now to interpret this idea in paint, in terms of space, color, line, texture, etc. I used a variety of technical means in this picture, bold strokes of the palette knife, with paint scraped off in places to get the rough texture of the foreground, in contrast to the smoother areas.

"The over-all composition is triangular, with the small figure in the right background establishing a space relationship with the foreground plane. In order to accent the loss of the soldier's leg, I drew the remaining foot large in the foreground, its direction related to the vertical plane of the bandaged arm. The receding triangular plane of the stretcher also emphasizes the foot in the foreground. And included in this total organization are the many things felt but not analyzed, which develop during the painting process."

ROBERT BENNEY: Just Off the Line. *Courtesy Abbott Collection of War Art*

Aaron Bohrod

"OAKDALE AVENUE IS a North Side street in Chicago on which I'd lived for several years before I began to paint this composition. I felt I was acquainted with all aspects of weather change in both day and evening when I chose a particular atmospheric envelopment to attend the familiar setting I wanted to express in paint.

"Fifteen years ago, when I began to work professionally, I had painted all the abstract and fantastic art out of my system and I had gone on to what I consider fuller and more important things. But I think I am still cognizant of the value of the abstract in determining the underlying design structure of a composition. My first sketches for this painting were almost non-objective allocations of the bulks and directions the later clothed forms of recognizable houses, trees, sky, and figure would take. With the design element established, I made more detailed sketches both in daytime and at night. And finally, with some deviation in appearance and in actual color tone whenever it was deemed necessary, but with a determination of firm adherence to the original feeling of the scene with its strange inner and outward aspects of artificial lighting, I brought the painting to completion in my studio.

"In all my painting I have chosen to work only from the elements of and the basic arrangements I can see in nature; or, in combination with the works of man. This I do with a greater or lesser faithfulness to actual appearance as I may desire. Because of my usual satisfaction with the forms nature has created, my deviations usually take the form of re-arrangement rather than that of radical distortion.

"I believe that only the constant refreshening that comes from a direct and humble approach to nature saves the artist from the inevitable sterility engendered by feeding constantly on his own trumped-up ideas, no matter how inventive or ingenious he may be."

AARON BOHROD: Oakdale Avenue at Night. *Collection of the Pennsylvania Academy of Fine Arts*

Louis Bosa

"IN THE PAINTING *Nuns Skating*, my concern was with expressing the religious motif in symbolic shapes and a mood of color to convey the soft music, the quiet, and the relaxation of sanctuary.

"The background is built up into a pyramid shape like a Gothic cathedral and the nun figures are developed in these same Gothic shapes. The tree, designed like the crucifixion, is intended to symbolize Christianity.

"The color key is low and sombre to express silence and seclusion even in the open air.

"The movement is restrained for a sense of dignity. There is a striving for drama in the opposition of the single nun moving in one direction and the group of three nuns close by moving in the opposite direction on the canvas. All the figures move in a circular path to give a sense of embrace; this circular movement is the theme of the composition.

"The slight suggestion of humor in the two nuns in the middle distance is intended to add a suggestion of human quality to the over-all spiritual quality of the canvas. The single figure at the left of the painting, arms outstretched, symbolizes the all-embracing church sheltering its children."

Louis Bosa: Nuns Skating. *Private collection, photograph courtesy Kleeman Gallery*

Morris Davidson

"THIS PICTURE IS an example of one of three types of painting which I practice. When I am interested primarily in abstraction I prefer to work with still-life forms and planes of space. When relationship of shapes and colors in a moving synthesis is the dominant drive the work that results is nonobjective and not abstract. The third category, of which *The Conversation* is typical, is an expression of a kind of humanism in which not individuals but symbols of human types are composed in a rhythmic and spatial organization in order to convey not an incident but a universal activity of humans. There are no models used, no individual characterizations, no setting, and hence no sense of immediacy. In all my figure compositions the effort is to use shapes related both to humans and to other living matter but not human anatomy as such. The purpose is to attain a cosmic feeling rather than describe a transitory emotion or incident. The color of course plays a large part in the attainment of this feeling and I doubt that a black and white reproduction can do more than merely indicate my intentions.

"In all my painting the underlying structural basis is the space organization and this is dependent not only upon the conception of the planes but upon their color relation. Color then serves a twofold purpose. It establishes the space tensions and engenders the psychological mood. In addition to this I am greatly interested in the expressiveness of surface, which no reproduction even in color could possibly convey."

Morris Davidson: The Conversation

Stuart Davis

"My work is generally regarded as Abstract. I do not regard it as such. All of my paintings, including the one here reproduced, are derived from specific subjects. This does not mean that I exclude any contextual ideas that occur to me in contemplating them. The result, of course, is never an objective report of the optical fact of the Subject. But it is an objective report of my experience and thought in relation to it.

"The Subject of *Pad #2* was a garden with a tree. The Y-shaped form in the center derived from that tree. To know this doesn't help matters any. I mention it merely to show how I anchor my creative excursion to a concrete object. The painting is divided horizontally into three parts. The upper part could be called 'the sky.' All kinds of things can happen in a sky: Events in it, and things that are not in it, but which cross it, and in that sense become part of it. What they were in this case are the usual things: clouds, leaves, telephone wires, horizon shapes, etc. I composed these freely from memory and imagination. The middle one of the three horizontal areas is what is commonly called 'the middle distance.' The bottom area is 'the foreground.' In these areas were a path, grass, fallen leaves, etc. I called these to mind in painting, and raised the impression to the level of Color-Space Logic. When impression of Subject is ideologically identified with the Color-Space terms of painting, you are liable to get something that is meant by the term 'Art.' If, on the other hand, what is sought is a theory about Art, you are certain to get what is generally meant by the term 'Abstract,' and I try very hard to avoid this."

Stuart Davis: Pad #2. *Photograph courtesy of the Downtown Gallery*

Vaughn Flannery

"I HAVE BEEN ASKED to explain why I painted *Preakness in Training;* especially why it was done in the particular manner in which it was painted. This question assumes that people—including painters—do things for reasons. I am not sure they do. Reasons are the alibis painters offer to justify having done what it pleased them to do.

"Preakness was a famous race horse. He won the Dinner Party Stakes back in the 1870's and gave his name to the Preakness Stakes run each spring by The Maryland Jockey Club at Pimlico. But why use this creature as the subject matter for a picture?

"I happen to like to breed, raise and race Thoroughbreds. I enjoy what I see around a race course and, to me, such a pleasure needs no justification.

"Now, I never laid eyes on Preakness. He lived, raced, and died nearly a quarter century before I was born. Preakness, as a subject, was simply an excuse to make up a picture. Into the picture I worked the visual aspects of racing that I recall most vividly. Once the subject was selected, my concern was in improvising a design that interested and pleased me. Obviously, I am a schematic painter but, truth is, my method is strictly trial and error.

"Actually, this picture is something I made up. It isn't real because it is a painting and all paintings are, *per se,* artificial. But it isn't unreal because it derives from reality.

"With all due respect to Preakness, he was only an excuse for making up a picture. Incidentally, down here in Maryland, we still use his name as an excuse to run a wonderful horse race each spring. The Preakness Stakes brings Marylanders a pleasant holiday; which pleasure, it might be added, citizens of The Free State find unnecessary to justify."

VAUGHN FLANNERY: Preakness in Training at Pimlico. *Phillips Memorial Gallery, Washington, D.C., photograph courtesy of the Kraushaar Galleries,*

Robert Gwathmey

"THE PAINTER'S CONCEPTION of the world about him must necessarily be interjected into his work. The fusion of this with the technical becomes the total realization.

"I am interested in pattern, defined shapes and their relation to one another, as opposed to atmospheric phenomena and fuzzy edges best expressed by impressionism. These shapes remain in their basic form and although embellished their essential oneness remains.

"The body which is tightly enclosed by the arms, remains a rectilinear entity although it includes the baby and broken sections that further define the body. In resolving the entire image all of the basic shapes have to connect and inter-relate. The rectilinear area of the skirt, formed by the pressure of the spread knees, is an oblong which creates an opposite movement in relation to the upright rectangle of the body. The association of similar shapes becomes apparent and they are further related and unified by the movement of the upper arms that carry into the extremities of the oblong. These two rectilinear shapes are both part of a third major area formed circularly by the thigh. This tying together is pronounced by the line of continuation coming from the arms and describing the thighs while continuing through the oblong.

"The other relation has to do with the figure and the background; a further extension of the relationship of the rectangles defined by the floor and the wall. The upright movement of the wall panels exaggerates the attenuation of the body and further expresses the architectural dignity of the figure. Finally, the lack of chiaroscuro allows for definite use of pattern, sharply placed color relations, and decided use of line.

"I believe in the affirmation and indivisibility of life and art. In seeking truth, a pre-requisite of all artists, I find that the depiction of a minority people as picturesque degenerates into romantic mockery. I've simply used the universal image of Madonna and Child."

ROBERT GWATHMEY: Lullaby. *Winner of Third Prize Third Annual Pepsi-Cola Art Competition*

John Haley

"THE ACT OF integrating an image of wild horses, mesa forms, and clouds began with the first move toward visualization. At first this was only a mental image acquired from a scene in the Indian country of New Mexico. Then followed the sketch (pencil), and finally, in indirection, adaptation of the subject to the material used (oil). The last part of the process took place in the studio and resulted not only in representation of the thing seen, but also in presentation of what was considered pictorially useful in things known about the subject.

"Perception of the subject was in terms of known pictorial possibilities and limitations. Casual or accidental movements of clouds, horses, and earth forms in nature became controlled and related movements in the picture. Triangular and elliptical shapes in larger and smaller divisions evolved and developed into rhythmical themes in the process of painting. Contrasts of spatial directions of horses, clouds, and earth forms contribute to the structure of movement. Undulating contours over the surface as well as vertical, horizontal, and diagonal divisions provide a decorative progression to relate areas further. Colors of the subjects were transposed to strengthen sequences of intensity and its opposite, to build up relation and balance across the surface of the painting, and to bring about climactic contrasts to punctuate one area of the surface in its effect upon another.

"The end result is that of forms and colors quite different from those in nature (sky is yellow, earth and clouds mostly blue) with the final effect dependent for its illusion of reality upon related fitness, and surprise through contrast, of one color to another as color, and upon the degree of importance that one form has for another and to the whole, as form. Thus objects which comprise the subject have become identified with one another in a decorative and spatial unity in which they acquire an importance to one another that is visually unlikely, if not impossible, in nature."

JOHN HALEY: Zuni Broomtails

Leah Rinne Hamilton

"In *Reunion* I was particularly interested in two elements of painting which I wished to explore and unite into a composition. These were the establishment of close and very deep space, and the juxtaposition of tangled forms against the larger patterns.

"Although the use of paint is rather two-dimensional, it was through the direction of line and contrast of values that an illusion of deep space was created. It was the intention that the eye move backward and forward in space as it does in normal observation.

"The floating objects, due to their size, are a tie between the smaller moving forms and the deep space. The clustering forms are primarily horizontal and vertical, placed against the more flowing large patterns. It is through this play in scale and movement that variety and tension are introduced both in space and textural quality. These forms have no tangible meaning aside from that which the observer wishes to supply.

"As the painting progressed the individual shapes, contours, and interlocking forms took their definition from preceding forms. In other words, it is the synthesis of the mood of the moment fused with the past experience of the artist."

LEAH RINNE HAMILTON: Reunion

Dong Kingman

"I BEGAN MY WATERCOLOR, *Old and New*, one Sunday morning near the Museum of Modern Art, not as a sketch but as a foundation for the final composition. The old studio buildings in the middle ground interested me, in contrast to the tall new buildings in the background, but lacked variety. So they were only indicated at the time, to be redesigned later in the studio.

"There were actually no signs on top of the buildings at the right; they were added to create space, and to act as linear forms against the softness of the smoke. The taller building on the left was intended to form a dynamic vertical line to break the monotony of the buildings alongside, while the shadow helps to create space between the back and middle planes, both shadows also acting as dynamic patterns of movement in an otherwise vertical composition. These shadows were compositionally placed, and do not result from a single source of light.

"The two stop signs are part of the space movement; the washing and signs on the buildings are used for their texture. The automobile and figures are intended to give movement and also add a humorous quality to an otherwise architectural subject.

"The old against the new, the complex against the simple, yin against yang, like and dislike, are the things I want to say in my pictures. I paint as I see, but also as I think."

DONG KINGMAN: Old and New. *Metropolitan Museum of Art, photograph courtesy Midtown Galleries*

Karl Knaths

"THE PARTICULAR PICTURE is not an isolated phenomenon but an outward manifestation of that particular link in the chain of events that constitute the painter's activity. This book will speak in its proper place of a definite order of design and the specific conventions in which it may be embodied. Thus to bring out my conception in this instance, a 'plane' convention was used. Planes were shifted and rotated in relation to the flat plane of the canvas, so that all were 'contained.' As an efficient contrast to the planes, calligraphic strokes were used. Out of the interplay of these means, as they moved themselves into groupings that finally resolved into a single composition, a composition that would reflect the particular feeling of trueness, thus beauty, to which I as the painter may have arrived.

"The canvas surface can give an indication of spaces and express things beyond the manner in which the eye receives an image upon the retina from nature. In all cases, from *trompe l'oeil* even up to Mondrian, there is selection, depending upon the particular thing the painter wishes to convey and which prescribes the choice of the convention used. This has been well stated by Penelope Redd in the *Pittsburgh Sun-Telegraph* in describing her impression of *Gear*: 'Karl Knaths has arrived at *Gear* after a long and lonely journey in overcoming the obstacles that detail throws into the path of an artist. Everything else in the world has been subjected to the rigors of summarization, so logically why not painting? Knaths' gulls are the essence of flight, his sea and sky and light suggest illimitable space, the power of nature. He has not depended upon color for drama but the organization of man's minutiae against infinity as perceived in nature. Not a single stroke could be eliminated because the whole is immutably integrated.'"

KARL KNATHS: Gear. *Winner of First Prize, Carnegie's "Painting in the United States, 1946"; photograph courtesy Paul Rosenberg & Co.*

Jacob Lawrence

"This painting, I approached in the same manner as I approach all of my work.

"First there is the subject—'Holy Stoning the Deck.'

"What is my reaction to this subject? What do I feel about the subject? Is it rhythmic; is it static; is it busy; is it quiet; and so on?

"Then I decide what feeling I wish to portray and what physical characteristics of the subject best sum up this feeling.

"All of my painting of this period had to do with men at sea during war and what they felt.

"In this painting I wanted to portray the feeling of men doing work in rhythm. By elongating the figures, drawing the figures to move and bend in the same direction, I hoped to achieve a certain rhythm. By interlocking the legs of the figures and the handles of the stones I hoped to achieve movement. I hoped to get even greater movement by the long horizontal lines that are part of the deck.

"In this painting I relied on composition rather than color to achieve my purpose. I hope I have been successful."

JACOB LAWRENCE: Holy Stoning the Deck. *Reproduction of Official Coast Guard Painting, photograph courtesy of the Museum of Modern Art, New York*

Ward Lockwood

"LATE AFTERNOON IN winter I started this painting 'on the spot' in a narrow street of adobe houses. After about two hours of work the representation of this particular street would have been recognizable to anyone familiar with the village but most of the work remained to be accomplished in the studio. It was necessary to heighten a color here, subdue one there; to bend one line and straighten another; to delete one form and reshape the next; to bind the composition horizontally by the image of a telephone pole; to balance one linear direction with another; and so forth until I felt all of the lines, colors, and shapes so related to each other and to the shape of the canvas that a meaningful unit of pictorial expression resulted.

"But perhaps this is just rationalization. A real explanation of the conscious and subconscious processes involved in the creation of a painting would be much more extensive—beyond my ability to recall or describe. The important fact is, however, that it is the artist's 'sense of rightness' which ultimately determines how successfully he uses pigments, brushes, 'hunches,' accidents, or theories in the execution of his work.

"There must exist in the observer also a reciprocal 'sense of rightness.' Reading about art, studying it, sleeping soundly, and eating good food may all help in the growth of this sense. But looking at works of art, many and many of them time and time again, and thus augmenting this particular sense *by and through the eye* is the all important *sine qua non* of real enjoyment and appreciation of art.

"But I am stealing your looking time, for if all the words written about art were laid end to end they would reach—and keep on reaching."

WARD LOCKWOOD: Street Scene, New Mexico

Erle Loran

"THE PAINTING IS a somewhat fantastic memory of Downieville in the Sierra Nevada Mountains. In this country the sun is dazzling and the air is sharp. I wanted to portray the brilliance and clarity of sunlight, not by light and shade but through an inner luminosity that should exude from the relationships that exist, in abstraction, in the colored surfaces of the painting. Pure black is used to create a large pattern interlocking the stream below with the exaggerated mountains above. The black areas serve as a foil for bright and contrasting warm and cool greens. By scraping and drawing into the colors an effect of translucency and clarity was intended to be still further developed.

"But it is embarrassing for the artist to write about his own work. If the subject matter is deeply personal he certainly will not reveal its meaning and in the case of a landscape, which is a portrayal of the objective world, no explanation of the subject seems necessary. A detailed analysis of the organization of design and color is likely to seem mathematical or technical and the artist is really not in a position to know what is most important in his own work regardless of what his aims or ideals may be.

"In *Mountain Village* the quality of light and the effect of space are obviously not based on chiaroscuro nor on linear and aerial perspective. Organization through a balanced distribution and interlocking of volume and color shapes was the aim. The observer alone can judge of the expressive and emotional effects that determine whether a painting is a vital, living unity. Naturally the artist always hopes to achieve rich emotional effects. The feeling might originally be based on a visual experience such as the view I saw at Downieville. To convey such an impression is an important element in the experience we call aesthetic; but it has no meaning as art unless it is moulded into a solid structure of planes and color shapes that come to life and remain balanced on the two-dimensional surface of the picture plane."

ERLE LORAN: Mountain Village. *San Francisco Museum of Art; Lloyd S. Ackerman, Jr., Memorial Fund*

Alice Trumbull Mason

"*Bearings in Transition* is the product of a number of themes carried out to the best of my ability and imagination. One theme is that of displacement of one form by another, every space in the painting being regarded as a separate form working in conjunction with all the others. Displacement should be understood in contradistinction to the idea of representing perspective on a two-dimensional plane. Displacement occurs through the juxtaposition of colors and through formal construction, that is, one form does not stand in front of another but displaces it with color and form. This concept is essential if one works, as I do, by using all four sides of the picture as a base.

"In general terms *Bearings in Transition* is a problem of direction and displacement motivated by a rhythmic shift of values constantly returning to the focal plane of the canvas.

"Specifically this painting deals with bearings in coordination with biomorphic and geometric forms, in which acute angles play a significant part. It was not constructed on the pyramid idea of heavy base and light top built up with volume and depth associations, but by a balance achieved by constantly turning the canvas around during the drawing and painting process. This necessitates, as I have said before, the concept at origin of displacement rather than volume construction.

"Direction in this painting is indicated through the play of bearings against other forms and its force is heightened by the use of close light and dark values with few intermediary tones, resulting in a consequent transposition and integration of direction with color quantities. The impetus of direction is implicit in the bearings. The rhythmic qualities of direction exist in the counteraction of other forms and are governed by the mood of the color."

ALICE TRUMBULL MASON: Bearings in Transition

Hobart Nichols

"*Tragedy*, THE PICTURE here reproduced, is the result of many observations of wrecked and abandoned homes in New England, particularly in New Hampshire and Vermont. The forlorn appearance of these old places stimulates a desire to reconstruct the story of their occupancy—the romance, the desire for security, the fulfilled ambition for a home and then the cruel frustration of hopes and finally the tragedy of failure and abandonment. Many of them are ideally located and still possess the charm that nature bestows so lavishly—blossoming fruit trees, vines gnarled and twisted to the toppling chimneys, flagstones embedded in green velvet moss and the old house in sad disrepair but beautiful in the patina made by the rains and frosts and blazing sun. One wonders why in such a place man failed. But this was obvious in the subject of my picture. Who could have hoped to survive the storms and rigor of bleak winter in such a location, perched on the summit of a mountain surrounded by uncompromising granite? Why did the man, perhaps with wife and children, dare risk his all under such handicaps? These were the thoughts that prompted the painting of *Tragedy*.

"I have traversed New England thoroughly, painting the attractive landscape, mountains, farmlands, and villages. They have an especial appeal to me from an objective point of view, but occasionally I am impressed from the purely humanistic side and *Tragedy* is an example.

"The picture was painted in the studio and is a composite of several sketches. The actual place does not exist. *Tragedy* was first exhibited in the National Academy's 117th Annual and received the Altman Prize. I have received poems and letters from people to whom the painting seemed to have a romantic appeal."

HOBART NICHOLS: Tragedy

Miné Okubo

"My sole purpose in painting is to make an interesting picture, simple in design and expression, and which presents a feeling of beauty in color and form. I do not attempt to depict realism but to probe beyond reality, to create something which is beautiful in itself.

"It is difficult for an artist to explain all that is involved in his creation, because the process of painting is a series of revelations and discoveries. For me, painting requires careful thought and planning, but the actual painting is spontaneous, a literal idea merely acting as a guide and stimulus. I begin with simple color shapes, developing the painting in this manner, and bringing the canvas to completion only when I feel that I have arrived at an interesting and satisfactory solution. In the process, the original idea may be lost by the development of more interesting shapes, for imagination is continually at work. Each painting is more or less an experiment rarely turning out as visualized, but discoveries are made to apply to future pictures.

"I began this canvas with the idea of painting a clown, and I thought about the circus world, of clowns, their laughter and gay activity. I tried to express this in an interesting design and not make a realistic painting. I painted only in terms of color, form, and design; subject matter was not the important thing in this painting. I do feel, however, that a painting which bears some relation to nature is more interesting, as it gives the artist an opportunity to interpret his own observation and experience."

Miné Okubo: Clown

I. Rice Pereira

"IN *White Lines* I have endeavored to explore the formal and design possibilities of painting, with special emphasis on constructional ways of expressing space on a two-dimensional surface, and experimenting with new materials and mediums. I have also tried to develop a working process using pigment itself to produce textural effects, vibrancy, luminosity, transparency, density of paint, the effect of light on incised and relief surfaces. *White Lines* employs actual textures as well as implied visual textural effects. The composition is held together with a network of white lines in semi-relief. Since this was one of the first experimental paintings on parchment, I used as many sympathetic and permanent mediums as possible since I wanted to determine the nature and reaction of the material as a painting surface. Different kinds of substances were used as well as numerous methods of applying pigment. Paint direct from the tube was used, as well as paint with fillers to create the semi-relief surfaces."

I. Rice Pereira: White Lines. *Collection of the Museum of Modern Art, New York*

Priscilla Roberts

"I CAN'T HELP FEELING that any illuminating remarks I might be able to make about my painting would seem somewhat beside the point, unless I can first justify my indulging in a rather widely discredited form of art.

"I have often been told that I should get a camera and save myself a lot of work. And I have always wished I had a pat excuse to give for not doing so. Because the truth is that the camera and I are both striving to achieve the same effect, which I believe is colloquially called 'total visual representation,' with most of the odds on the side of the camera. And all the arguments which have so far been thought up to prove a painter can do something a photographer can't, seem to take it for granted that the painter is deliberately trying to do something the photographer isn't, by interpreting, rather than directly rendering, his subject matter.

"To an ever-inquiring mind this sounds just the least little bit as though painting had gallantly met the challenge of photography by turning tail and fleeing. But anyone who feels the need of justifying his craving for pictorial expression will probably not question his rationalization too closely—unless what he's really looking for is a good excuse for not painting. And provided one doesn't hesitate to adapt it to one's individual requirements, a plausible rationalization has its uses—I might even invoke one myself by palming off my shortcomings as artistic interpretations, should I be told to get a camera once too often. But for my own peace of mind I feel the need of neither a justification nor a camera to save me work and incidentally do me out of a most enthralling occupation."

PRISCILLA ROBERTS: Interior. *Photograph courtesy of the Grand Central Galleries, Inc., New York*

Vaclav Vytlacil

"I HAVE DEFINITELY committed myself to paint-
ing pictures that will, I hope, radiate a state of 'well being.' This may well
remain my task for a long time to come. It is as simple as that. I am
anxious to eliminate all heavy intellectualisms and ponderous esthetic
theories. These are the roots, vital and necessary; but do we not all prefer
the flower? How wonderful it would be to paint as simply as the children
paint, and with equal intensity and enjoyment. Would not others be able
to partake of this enjoyment? I believe the answer to be, Yes. I would
like to submerge my entire personality so completely in my painting that
none of it remains outside of the picture; and in so doing I will have,
in my opinion, done my job, as I see it.

"In *Fisherman's Cove* I have taken a number of shapes derived from a
New England fishing boat, the little town, water, waves, and sky. I have
tried to weave them quite freely into an ornamental pattern. My belief
is that through this pattern the subjects speak more emotionally and
dramatically than they do in their literal singleness."

Vaclav Vytlacil: Fisherman's Cove. *Photograph courtesy Feigl Gallery*

Glenn Wessels

"*Oil Wells: Los Angeles* was painted partly on the spot (which is alongside the car line to Glendale) and partly in the studio. A big yellow oil truck continued an arabesque line which bound up the background of gardens and houses on the hill with the oil apparatus in the foreground. The view suggested a space-pattern rhythm with an emotional tone which I felt I could develop. An underpainting of thin, transparent color first set down the main features of the composition, and the final developments were carried out in opaque, covering gouache. My gouache palette consists mainly of mixtures of pigment powder with a mucilage binding, prepared by myself because I believe that qualities of color and texture may thus be more readily controlled than by the use of tube colors alone.

"There were a great many small forms in this subject and they would have been chaotic and confusing to an observer if they had not been grouped in the painting into larger unities. For instance, the oil derrick is painted as a single color-shape, with the details of the timbers subordinated to the whole. These smaller unities are also grouped and adjusted in relation to each other so that a simpler, more geometrical order appears, and so that a balance across the optical center of the format might be achieved.

"The relations subjectively felt between shapes were sometimes indicated by drawn lines, or emphasized by allowing the linear textures of the brush strokes to show. In general the brush follows that axis of a plane which is the important direction for that particular plane to emphasize in relation to the rest of the picture. Such leading textures may be seen in the foreground planes in this picture.

"I enjoyed making this painting, because I enjoy painting and I'm interested in oil wells and like the smell of oil."

GLENN WESSELS: Oil Wells: Los Angeles. *Collection of the Seattle Art Museum*

Pictures without Words: Which Do You Like?

SEVERAL PAGES OF pictures follow, pictures without titles, without painters' names, without historic associations or other information usually thought to belong to pictures. In looking at these, as pictures without words, you will be able to make your own decisions as to how they affect *you*.

It is of no importance that not all pictures are great works of art, but it is important to understand what even a minor picture has to say, and to enjoy it accordingly. Picture titles, painters' and owners' names, and like information will be found on page 268.

1

2

3

4

5

6

7

8

9

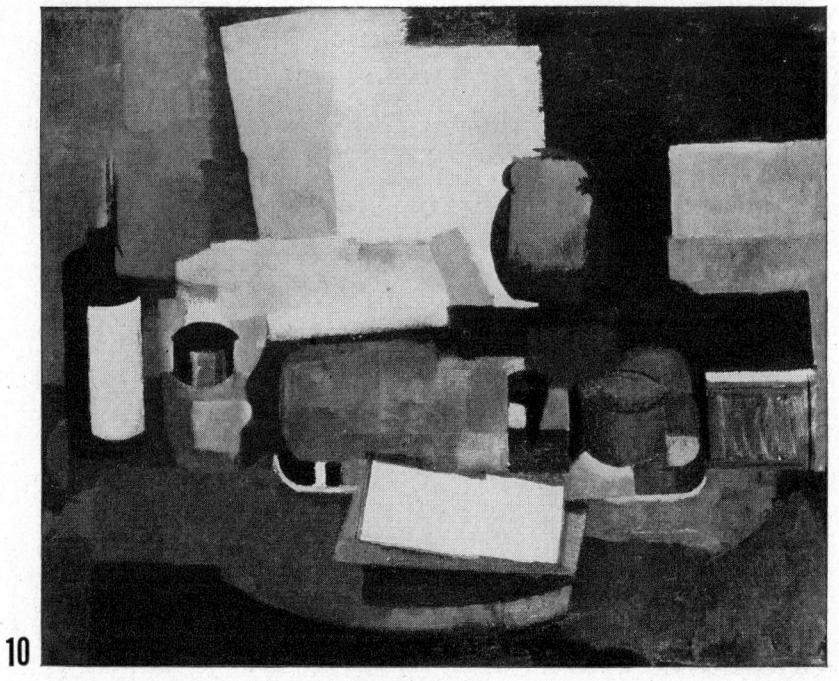

10

Words about the Pictures

1. W. N. HARNETT: The Old Cremona. *Courtesy of the Metropolitan Museum of Art*
2. GIOVANNI DI PAOLO: Paradise. *Courtesy of the Metropolitan Museum of Art*
3. PAUL KLEE: Boats in the Evening Sun. *Courtesy of the Nierendorf Gallery*
4. MING DYNASTY: Detail from a Chinese Painting. *Courtesy of the Metropolitan Museum of Art*
5. JEAN HUGO: Les Deux Orphélines. *Photograph courtesy of Mr. Ludwig Charell*
6. BOLTON JONES: Spring. *Courtesy of the Metropolitan Museum of Art*
7. JEAN CHARLOT: Woman Lifting Rebozo. *Collection of the Museum of Modern Art, New York*
8. JOSEPH SCHARL: Loaves of Bread. *Courtesy of the Nierendorf Gallery*
9. W. RANFORD KEEFE (?): Tree of Foreboding. *Courtesy of the Harry Stone Gallery*
10. ROGER DE LA FRESNAYE: Still Life. *Collection of the Museum of Modern Art, New York*

The Summing Up

Y OU HAVE LOOKED at many reproductions of pictures, and found numerous attempts to clarify different ideas, some of which may have been new to you. You have agreed with some, and disagreed with others. Some of the pictures you have liked, and some you have not. My endeavor has been to aid you in seeing more completely, to give you some of the reasons why painters paint as they do. It is now up to you, and for *your* enjoyment only, to look and feel a little more intensely when looking at a work of art, or if the picture represents a literary or factual point of view, to recognize it for what it is, and enjoy it in that way.

This book is incomplete, as art itself is always incomplete; there's always something more to be said, and always someone to say it.

I have, in a sense, taken pictures apart, and concentrated on these isolated ideas. It is now up to you to put them together again, in your own way. After all is said and done, you'll continue to make one of two comments about any picture:

"I like it."

"I don't like it."

But that decision will not be final; your future point of view may change. And your choice will always be your own, no matter what anyone else may say, do, or think.

> Be she fairer than the day
>   Or the flowery meads in May,
> If she be not so to me,
>   What care I how fair she be?
>
> —*George Wither* (*1588-1667*)

BIBLIOGRAPHY

Cubists and Post-Impressionism
Arthur Jerome Eddy
A. C. McClurg & Co.
Chicago, 1919

La Peinture Moderne
Ozenfant and Jeanneret
Les Éditions G. Crés & Cie.
Paris

Summa Artis
El Arte Prehistorico Europeo
José Pijoán
Espasa-Calpe, S.A.
Madrid, 1934

How to See Modern Pictures
Ralph M. Pearson
The Dial Press
New York, 1925

Aesthetic Quality
Stephen C. Pepper
Charles Scribner's Sons
New York, 1938

Language of Vision
Gyorgy Kepes
Paul Theobald
Chicago, 1944

Psychological Optics
Samuel Renshaw, M.A., Ph.D.
Optometric Extension Program
Duncan, Oklahoma, 1942

The History of Impressionism
John Rewald
The Museum of Modern Art
New York, 1946

The Problem of Form
Adolf Hildebrand
G. E. Stechert & Co.
New York, 1932

Painting for Pleasure
Morris Davidson
Hale, Cushman & Flint
Boston, 1938

Artists on Art
Robert Goldwater and
 Marco Treves
Pantheon Books, Inc.
New York, 1945

Basic Principles of Painting
Glenn A. Wessels
University of California, 1946

What is Modern Painting?
Alfred H. Barr, Jr.
The Museum of Modern Art
New York, 1943

Cézanne's Composition
Erle Loran
University of California Press,
 1943

[270]

INDEX

[273]

space combined with, 98, 99
staccato, 110
Pearson, Ralph M., 16
Pêcheurs à la Ligne, Les, Dufy, 94
Pennsylvania Academy of Fine Arts, 221
Pepsi-Cola Art Competition, 231
Pereira, I. Rice, 252, 253
Perls Galleries, 61, 94, 161, 191
Perspective, 88
  Chinese treatment, 96
  defined, 50
  East Indian treatment, 96, 97
  faults of, 94, 95
  mechanical, 92
Phillips Memorial Gallery, 229
Photographs and photography, 12, 13,
    110, 216, 217
  art and, 20, 55, 254
  contributions, 22
  designed, 22
  influence on illustration, 32
  light and shade, 82, 83
  limitations, 22
  motif, 104, 105, 115-137
  nude in, 68, 69
  painting and, 20, 55, 254
Picasso, Pablo, 71, 74-77, 137, 206, 207
PICASSO: FORTY YEARS OF HIS ART, ed.
    Barr, 206
PICASSO, THE RECENT YEARS, Harriet and
    Sidney Janis, 136, 137
Pictographs, 6, 7
Picture plane, defined, 50
  space and, 88, 89
Pictures, actual world and, 106-107
  broad divisions of, 138
  darks in, 82
  defined, 164
  emotion in, 32, 56
  evolution of, 54-56, 71-77
  explaining, 3
  explanatory notes, 215-259
  historical, 46
  how painted, 54-56, 71-77
  information in, 12, 55, 56
  lights in, 82
  literary, 26, 27, 42
  movement in, 20, 55
  preference, 18
  realistic, 32
  story-telling, 26, 27, 42
  subjects and, 18
  unlabeled, 261-267

variation in meanings, 11
words and, 6
PICTURES AT AN EXHIBITION, Mussorg-
    sky, 36
Pinacoteca Vanucci, 145
Pissarro, Camille, 123
Planes, 88
  defined, 50
  idea of, 90
  in space, 111
  (*see also* Picture plane)
Portinari, Candido, 151
Portrait d'une Jeune Fille, Modigliani,
    161
Portrait of a Lady, van der Weyden, 165,
    167
Portraits, 48, 49
Prado, 155, 181
Preakness in Training at Pimlico, Flan-
    nery, 228, 229
Propaganda in Art, 44
Proportion, 140

Rainy Day, Cowles, 169
Realism, 64
  development to abstraction, 78-79, 115-
    137
Recession and return, 111
Recognition, Naval, 14-15
Redd, Penelope, 238
Reindeer, cave painting, 61
Renoir, Pierre Auguste, 40, 41
Renshaw, Samuel, 15
Reunion, Hamilton, 234, 235
Rewald, John, v, 105, 118, 120, 122,
    124
Rey, Robert, 196
Rhythm, 80
Ribak, Louis, 49
Richmond Child Care Center, 188, 189
Roberts, Priscilla, 254, 255
Robinson, Boardman, 141
Rochers à Belle-Isle, Monet, 121
Rosenberg (Paul) and Company, 43, 238,
    239
Route Tournante, La, Cézanne, 105
St. Nicholas and the Three Youths,
    Lorenzo, 138, 139
San Francisco Museum of Art, 144, 245
Scarecrow, Portinari, 151
Scharl, Joseph, 266, 268
Schiefer, Johannes, 158, 159
Science, art and, 60

[275]

[276]